# Ninja Air Fryer Cookbook UK

*Delicious & Amazing Ninja Dual Zone Air Fryer Recipes For Family & Friends | Meat, Poultry, Desserts & More | Beginner Tips & Tricks To Make Your Meals Taste Fabulous*

WILLIAM G. CHARLES

ISBN - 9798856693781

# Table of Contents

# EXCLUSIVE BONUS

## 40 Weight Loss Recipes

## &

## 14 Days Meal Plan

Scan the QR-Code and receive
the FREE download:

# Introduction to air frying

This cookbook is perfect for anyone who wants to eat healthy but still enjoy delicious food!

Air frying is a revolutionary cooking method that allows you to enjoy your favourite fried foods without all the added oil and fat. This cookbook is a collection of delicious and nutritious recipes from different cuisines around the world, including Asian, Mediterranean, and American, that will help you lead a healthy lifestyle, and enjoy doing so!

What is an air fryer? An air fryer is a kitchen appliance that uses hot air to cook food. It circulates hot air around the food, creating a crispy exterior similar to deep-frying, but with less oil. This can result in healthier versions of fried foods. They come in a variety of sizes and can be used to cook a wide range of foods, including meat, vegetables, and French fries.

The recipes in this cookbook are specially curated to showcase the versatility of air frying and the variety of flavours that can be achieved with this method. From crispy chicken wings and sweet potato fries to healthy fish and vegetable dishes, there is something for everyone. Each recipe in this cookbook includes detailed instructions and helpful tips to ensure that your food comes out perfectly every time. You'll also find nutritional information for each recipe, so you can make informed choices about what you're eating.

Some of the delicious and nutritious recipes that you'll find in this cookbook include:

- Air Fryer Chicken Parmesan: Chicken breast coated in a smooth marinara sauce and mozzarella cheese makes for a mouthwatering and satisfying dinner.
- Air Fryer BBQ Baby Back Ribs: Chicken: A sweet and savoury dish made with BBQ sauce and air fried to perfection.

- Air Fryer Sweet Potato Fries: A healthy alternative to traditional French fries made with sweet potatoes and a sprinkle of sea salt.

- Air Fryer Shrimp La Bang Bang: A light and flavourful dish made with crispy shrimp and coated in a sweet and spicy sauce.

- Air Fryer Apricot and Apple Crisp: With its warm and gooey fruit filling and crispy and buttery topping, it will have your taste buds doing the cha-cha.

# About Ninja Dual Zone air fryer

Our recipes are made using the Ninja Dual Zone air fryer, a powerful and versatile kitchen appliance that allows you to cook two different types of food at different temperatures and times simultaneously. Featuring two independent cooking zones, each with its own temperature control and timer, allowing you to cook different types of food at the same time without any flavour transfer. The unit also comes with a dehydrate function and the non-stick ceramic-coated basket and crisper plate are dishwasher safe and the unit itself is easy to clean. With its dual-zone design, large capacity, and easy to clean design, the Ninja Dual Zone air fryer allows any kitchen to cook different types of food at the same time.

The Ninja Dual Zone air fryer is a revolutionary kitchen appliance that has changed the way people think about healthy eating. This air fryer utilizes a unique dual zone technology that allows for the cooking of two different foods at the same time, without any cross-contamination of flavours or smells. This means that you can cook your favourite fried foods, such as French fries or chicken wings, while also cooking a healthy side dish, such as vegetables or fish.

One of the major advantages of the Ninja Dual Zone air fryer is its ability to cook food with little to no oil, which makes it a healthier alternative to traditional frying methods. The air fryer uses hot air to circulate around the food, creating a crispy and delicious crust while keeping the inside moist and juicy. This results in food that is healthier and lower in calories, without sacrificing flavour or texture.

Another great feature of the Ninja Dual Zone air fryer is its versatility. It can be used to cook a wide variety of foods, from frozen snacks to fresh vegetables and meats. It also has a variety of cooking settings and preset options, such as the "air fry" setting for crispy foods, and the "roast" setting for meats and vegetables. This allows you to easily cook a wide variety of meals, without having to worry about adjusting the temperature or timing.

In addition to its versatility and health benefits, the Ninja Dual Zone air fryer is also very easy to use and clean. It has a large, non-stick cooking basket and a removable drip tray that make it easy to clean up after cooking. It also has a digital touch screen display that allows you to easily set the temperature, cooking time, and mode, and monitor the cooking progress.

Compared to other air fryers on the market, the Ninja Dual Zone air fryer stands out for its unique dual zone technology, which allows for the cooking of two different foods at the same time, without any cross-contamination of flavour or smells. This is a feature that is not found in other air fryers, and it makes the Ninja Dual Zone air fryer a great option for people who want to cook multiple dishes at the same time, or who want to cook different types of food without having to worry about cross-contamination.

Overall, the Ninja Dual Zone air fryer is a game-changing kitchen appliance that has revolutionized the way people think about healthy eating. Its unique dual zone technology, versatility, and ease of use make it a great option for anyone looking to cook delicious, healthy meals at home. It's a great investment for those looking to make healthy eating easy and convenient in their kitchen and the Ninja brand is known for quality and durability.

The XXL Ninja air fryer is also a great investment that allows you to cook a variety of foods with little to no oil. This air fryer has a large 5.5-quart capacity, making it perfect for cooking meals for the whole family. The unit features a digital display, a wide temperature range and a timer for precision cooking. The Ninja air fryer XL also has a unique "air crisp" technology that circulates hot air around the food, resulting in crispy and evenly cooked meals. In addition, the air fryer includes a multi-layer rack to cook multiple items at once and a removable, dishwasher-safe basket for easy cleaning.

# Health benefits

Cooking with an air fryer has become increasingly popular in recent years, and for good reason. Not only is it a quick and easy way to prepare food, but it also offers a number of health benefits. In this chapter, we will explore some of the key benefits of cooking with an air fryer and how it can help improve your overall health.

One of the most significant benefits of cooking with an air fryer is that it allows you to prepare food with little to no oil. Traditional deep-frying methods require a large amount of oil, which can add a significant amount of calories and unhealthy fats to your food. Air fryers, on the other hand, use hot air to circulate around the food, cooking it to perfection while using minimal oil or none at all. This means that you can enjoy your favourite fried foods without the added guilt of consuming excessive amounts of oil.

Another benefit of cooking with an air fryer is that it can help to reduce the risk of certain diseases. Studies have shown that consuming a diet high in saturated fats and trans fats can increase the risk of heart disease, stroke, and other chronic health conditions. By cooking with an air fryer, you can significantly reduce your intake of these unhealthy fats and improve your overall health. Air fryers also offer the benefit of being able to cook food at high temperatures without the fear of harmful smoke or fumes.

In addition to the health benefits, cooking with an air fryer also offers a number of convenience benefits. One of the main advantages is that it is much faster than traditional deep-frying methods. Because the hot air circulates around the food, it cooks faster and more evenly. This means that you can have your food ready in a fraction of the time it would take to prepare it using traditional methods.

Another convenience benefit is that air fryers are very easy to clean. Most models come with non-stick baskets and trays that can be easily removed and washed in the dishwasher. This means that you can spend less time cleaning up and more time enjoying your food.

Air fryers also offer a wide range of cooking options. Many models come with multiple cooking functions, such as baking, roasting, and dehydrating. This means that you can use your air fryer to prepare a wide variety of dishes, including chicken, fish, vegetables, and even desserts.

In conclusion, cooking with an air fryer offers a number of health and convenience benefits. By using minimal oil or none at all, you can enjoy your favourite fried foods without the added guilt of consuming excessive amounts of oil. Air fryers can also help to reduce the risk of certain diseases, are safe to use and produce no smoke or fumes. They are also faster and easier to clean than traditional deep-frying methods and offer a wide range of cooking options. Overall, an air fryer is a great addition to any kitchen, and a great way to improve your overall health.

# Why air fry?

Air frying vs deep frying

Deep frying is a popular method of cooking that involves submerging food in hot oil. While it can create delicious and crispy foods, it also poses significant health risks. In this part, we will explore some of the key health problems associated with deep frying food.

One of the main health risks associated with deep frying is the high calorie content of the food. When food is submerged in hot oil, it absorbs a significant amount of oil, which can add a significant amount of calories and unhealthy fats to the food. Consuming a diet high in saturated fats and trans fats can increase the risk of heart disease, stroke, and other chronic health conditions.

Another health risk associated with deep frying is the formation of harmful compounds during the cooking process. When oil is heated to high temperatures, it can produce harmful compounds such as acrolein and acrylamide. These compounds have been linked to an increased risk of cancer and other health problems.

Deep frying increases the risk of food contamination. When oil is reused multiple times, it can lead to the formation of harmful bacteria and other microorganisms that can cause food poisoning. Furthermore, if the oil is not stored or handled properly, it can become rancid and produce off-flavours and odours that can affect the quality and taste of the food.

Deep frying can also lead to problems with the respiratory system. The smoke and fumes produced by deep-frying methods can be harmful to the lungs and can aggravate respiratory conditions such as asthma and bronchitis. It can also cause eye, nose and throat irritations.

Another problem associated with deep frying is the risk of burns and scalds. Hot oil can cause severe burns and scalds if it comes into contact with the skin, and can also cause fires if not handled properly.

Finally, deep frying can be a time-consuming and messy process. It requires a large amount of oil, which can be difficult to store and dispose of, and it can be a hassle to clean up after cooking.

In conclusion, deep frying is a popular method of cooking that can create delicious and crispy foods, but it also poses significant health risks. It increases the risk of heart disease, cancer, and other health problems, can cause food contamination and respiratory problems, and it can be a time-consuming and messy process. If you enjoy fried foods, it's important to be aware of these risks and consider alternative cooking methods such as air frying.

# Healthy living starts in the kitchen

Living a healthy lifestyle begins in the kitchen. What we eat plays a crucial role in our overall health and well-being, and the choices we make in the kitchen can have a significant impact on our physical, mental, and emotional health. In this article, we will explore how healthy living starts in the kitchen and the steps we can take to improve our health through the food we eat.

One of the most important aspects of healthy living is maintaining a balanced diet. This means consuming a variety of different foods from all food groups, including fruits, vegetables, whole grains, lean proteins, and healthy fats. A balanced diet provides the body with all the essential nutrients it needs to function properly, including vitamins, minerals, and antioxidants. Eating a variety of different foods also helps to ensure that we are consuming a wide range of nutrients and helps to reduce the risk of nutrient deficiencies.

Another important aspect of healthy living is eating nutrient-dense foods. This means choosing foods that are high in nutrients and low in calories. Foods such as fruits, vegetables, whole grains, and lean proteins are nutrient-dense and provide the body with essential nutrients while also helping to keep calorie intake in check.

Preparing meals at home is another key aspect of healthy living. When we cook at home, we have control over the ingredients we use and can ensure that we are using healthy, whole foods. We can also control the amount of salt, sugar, and unhealthy fats that we add to our food, which can help to reduce the risk of chronic health conditions such as heart disease, diabetes, and obesity.

Eating a plant-based diet is also beneficial for health. Plant-based diets are high in fibre, vitamins, and minerals, and are low in saturated fats and cholesterol. They are also associated with a lower risk of heart disease, diabetes, and certain types of cancer.

Another important aspect of healthy living is being mindful of portion sizes. Consuming large portions of food can lead to weight gain and other health problems. By paying attention to portion sizes, we can ensure that we are consuming the right amount of food to meet our energy needs without overdoing it.

In addition to what we eat, how we eat is also important. Eating at a leisurely pace, not multitasking while eating, and paying attention to hunger and fullness cues can help us to eat mindfully and make healthier food choices.

Finally, it's important to keep in mind that healthy living is not just about what we eat but also about the overall lifestyle. This includes regular physical activity, getting enough sleep, managing stress, and avoiding smoking and excessive alcohol consumption.

By making healthy food choices, cooking at home, eating mindfully, and being aware of portion sizes, we can improve our overall health and well-being. Additionally, a balanced diet, a plant-based diet, and incorporating physical activity and good sleep hygiene are also important for overall health. Making small changes in the kitchen can have a big impact on our health and well-being, and it's never too late to start making healthier choices.

**Note: Cooking time may vary depending on the brand and model of your air fryer. The nutrition facts will vary depending on the brand of ingredients used.**

# EXCLUSIVE BONUS

## 40 Weight Loss Recipes

## &

## 14 Days Meal Plan

Scan the QR-Code and receive
the FREE download:

# Recipes – Breakfast

# Blueberry Porridge

This recipe for Blueberry Porridge in an air fryer is a delicious and healthy breakfast option that's perfect for busy mornings. Made with fresh blueberries, oats, and milk, this recipe is a tasty way to start your day and get some essential nutrients. Plus, it's a fun and easy twist on the traditional porridge recipe.

**NUTRITION PER SERVING:**
CALORIES: 400
FAT: 10G
CARBOHYDRATES: 70G
PROTEIN: 12G

**PREPARATION TIME:** 5 MINS
**COOK TIME:** 10 MINS

## INGREDIENTS:

- 150g blueberries
- 150g rolled oats
- 300ml milk
- 1 tablespoon vanilla extract
- 2 tablespoons honey
- Cooking spray

## INSTRUCTIONS:

1. Preheat your air fryer to 180°C, for 5 minutes.
2. In a mixing bowl, combine the rolled oats, milk, vanilla extract, honey, and blueberries.
3. Lightly coat the air fryer basket with cooking spray and pour the oatmeal mixture into the basket.
4. Cook in the air fryer for 8-10 minutes or until the oatmeal is heated through and the blueberries are slightly softened.
5. Serve and enjoy!

# Bacon and Egg Breakfast Muffins

## SERVES 4

Fancy some Bacon and Egg Breakfast Muffins? This recipe is a quick and easy way to enjoy a classic breakfast dish. Made with bacon, eggs, and muffin mix, this recipe is perfect for busy mornings or as a quick and easy breakfast option.

**NUTRITION PER SERVING:**
CALORIES: 240
FAT: 14G
CARBOHYDRATES: 18G
PROTEIN: 10G

PREPARATION TIME: 5 MINS
COOK TIME: 10 MINS

## INGREDIENTS:

- 4 slices of bacon (80g)
- 4 eggs
- 120g muffin mix
- 120ml milk
- Cooking spray

## INSTRUCTIONS:

1. Preheat your air fryer to 180°C, for 5 minutes.
2. In a mixing bowl, combine the muffin mix and milk.
3. Crack one egg into each of the 4 cups of a muffin tin and wrap a slice of bacon around the edge of each cup.
4. Pour the muffin mixture into each cup, filling about 2/3 of the way.
5. Place the muffin tin in the air fryer basket and cook for 8-10 minutes or until a toothpick inserted into the centre of a muffin comes out clean.
6. Serve and enjoy!

# French Toast Sticks

Perfect for a weekend brunch or a quick and satisfying breakfast on the go. This dish is made with slices of bread, beaten eggs, milk, and a touch of cinnamon, and it's cooked to golden-brown perfection in an air fryer. The result is a crispy exterior and a warm, fluffy interior that's sure to delight your taste buds. Whether you're looking for a classic comfort food or something a little different, this air-fried French toast is sure to please. So, let's get started!

**NUTRITION PER SERVING:**
CALORIES: 230
FAT: 8G
CARBOHYDRATES: 29G
PROTEIN: 8G

PREPARATION TIME: 5 MINS
COOK TIME: 10 MINS

## INGREDIENTS:

- 4 slices of white bread (about 200g)
- 2 eggs
- 120ml milk
- 1 tablespoon vanilla extract
- 1 tablespoon sugar
- Cooking spray

## INSTRUCTIONS:

1. Preheat your air fryer to 180°C, for 5 minutes.
2. Cut the bread slices into strips.
3. In a mixing bowl, whisk together the eggs, milk, vanilla extract, and sugar.
4. Dip each bread strip into the egg mixture, ensuring that both sides are coated.
5. Lightly coat the air fryer basket with cooking spray and place the bread strips in the basket.
6. Cook in the air fryer for 8-10 minutes or until golden brown and crispy.
7. Serve and enjoy!

# Hash Browns

If you're looking for a crispy and delicious breakfast option, look no further than this recipe for air-fried hash browns. Made with grated potatoes, a touch of oil, and a sprinkle of salt and pepper, these hash browns are cooked to perfection in an air fryer. The result is a crispy exterior and a warm, tender interior that's sure to please. This recipe is perfect for a quick breakfast or brunch, and it's a great way to use up leftover potatoes. It's also a great option for those who want to make a healthier version of the traditional fried hash browns. So, let's get started!

**NUTRITION PER SERVING:**
CALORIES: 150
FAT: 10G
CARBOHYDRATES: 12G
PROTEIN: 2G

PREPARATION TIME: 5 MINS
COOK TIME: 10 MINS

## INGREDIENTS:

- 1 large potato (about 250g)
- 1 tablespoon vegetable oil
- Salt and pepper, to taste

## INSTRUCTIONS:

1. Preheat your air fryer to 180°C, for 5 minutes.
2. Peel and grate the potato into small pieces.
3. In a mixing bowl, toss the grated potato with the vegetable oil, salt, and pepper.
4. Place the mixture in the air fryer basket and cook for 10-12 minutes or until golden brown and crispy.
5. Serve and enjoy!

# Strawberry Oatmeal

### SERVES 4

Get ready for a breakfast treat that's out of this world! This recipe for air-fried strawberry oatmeal is the perfect way to start your day. It's a fun and delicious way to enjoy all the flavours of fresh strawberries, combined with the wholesome goodness of oatmeal. The air fryer gives the oatmeal a crispy crust, while the inside stays warm and creamy. It's a great way to enjoy a healthy and tasty breakfast, whether you're in a rush or have some extra time to enjoy your morning meal. So, let's get our air fryers ready and make this delicious recipe!

**NUTRITION PER SERVING:**
CALORIES: 250
FAT: 5G
CARBOHYDRATES: 45G
PROTEIN: 7G

PREPARATION TIME: 5 MINS
COOK TIME: 10 MINS

## INGREDIENTS:

- 150g fresh strawberries, hulled and diced
- 150g rolled oats
- 150ml milk
- 50g sugar
- 1 tablespoon vanilla extract
- Cooking spray

## INSTRUCTIONS:

1. Preheat your air fryer to 180°C, for 5 minutes.
2. In a mixing bowl, combine the rolled oats, milk, sugar, vanilla extract, and diced strawberries.
3. Lightly coat the air fryer basket with cooking spray and pour the oatmeal mixture into the basket.
4. Cook in the air fryer for 8-10 minutes or until the oatmeal is heated through and the strawberries are slightly softened.
5. Serve and enjoy!

   Note: You can adjust the amount of sugar depending on your preference.

# Sausage and Pancakes

### SERVES 4

This recipe for Sausage and Pancakes in an air fryer is a delicious and easy breakfast option that's perfect for busy mornings. Made with just a few simple ingredients, this recipe combines savoury sausages and fluffy pancakes for a satisfying meal that's sure to please the whole family.

**NUTRITION PER SERVING:**
CALORIES: 520
FAT: 35G
CARBOHYDRATES: 32G
PROTEIN: 21G

PREPARATION TIME: 5 MINS
COOK TIME: 10 MINS

## INGREDIENTS:

○ 150g sausages (your choice of flavour)
○ 150g pancake mix
○ 150ml water
○ Cooking spray

## INSTRUCTIONS:

1. Preheat your air fryer to 180°C, for 5 minutes.
2. In a mixing bowl, combine the pancake mix and water until smooth.
3. Lightly coat the sausages with cooking spray and place them in the air fryer basket.
4. Pour the pancake batter over the sausages.
5. Cook in the air fryer for 8-10 minutes or until the pancakes are golden brown and the sausages 6. are cooked through.
6. Serve and enjoy!

   Note: You can adjust the amount of pancake mix and water depending on the size of your air fryer basket.

# Blueberry Oatmeal Banana Bites

## SERVES 4

These Blueberry Oatmeal Banana Bites are the perfect solution for breakfast! Made with ripe bananas, fresh blueberries, and rolled oats, these bites are packed with flavour and nutrition. The air fryer gives them a crispy exterior and warm inside, making them a perfect on-the-go breakfast option.

You can make a batch on Sunday and enjoy them all week long. This recipe is perfect for both kids and adults, it's gluten-free, and can be easily made vegan. So, let's gather our ingredients and make this delicious breakfast treat! The following recipe makes 8-10 bites and takes about 10 minutes to prepare and cook.

**NUTRITION PER SERVING:**
CALORIES: 170
FAT: 12G
CARBOHYDRATES: 2G
PROTEIN: 12G

PREPARATION TIME: 5 MINS
COOK TIME: 10 MINS

## INGREDIENTS:

- 2 ripe bananas (about 200g)
- 125g of rolled oats
- 30g of all-purpose flour (all-purpose or whole wheat)
- 60g of blueberries (fresh or frozen)
- 30ml of honey
- 1/2 teaspoon of cinnamon
- Cooking spray

## INSTRUCTIONS:

1. Preheat your air fryer to 180°C, for 5 minutes.
2. In a mixing bowl, mash the bananas until smooth.
3. Stir in the rolled oats, all-purpose flour, blueberries, honey and cinnamon.
4. Using a spoon or cookie scoop, form the mixture into bite-sized balls.
5. Lightly spray the air fryer basket with cooking spray.
6. Place the bites in the basket, making sure to not overcrowd them.
7. Cook for 8-10 minutes or until golden brown and crispy on the outside.
8. Serve and enjoy!

    Note: You can add more honey or cinnamon depending on your taste preference. Also, you can use almond all-purpose flour or gluten-free flour if you prefer.

# Breakfast Frittata

## SERVES 4

Breakfast Frittata is a versatile dish that can be made in an air fryer. It's a perfect option for a quick and healthy breakfast, brunch or even dinner. The following recipe Serves 4 people and takes about 15 minutes to prepare and cook.

**NUTRITION PER SERVING:**
CALORIES: 180
FAT: 10G
CARBOHYDRATES: 4G
PROTEIN: 13G

PREPARATION TIME: 5 MINS
COOK TIME: 10 MINS

## INGREDIENTS:

- ○ 8 eggs
- ○ 125ml of milk
- ○ Salt and pepper, to taste
- ○ 120g of diced vegetables such as bell peppers, onions, mushrooms, and tomatoes
- ○ 60g of diced cooked ham or bacon
- ○ 30g of grated cheese (cheddar or mozzarella)
- ○ Cooking spray

## INSTRUCTIONS:

1. Preheat your air fryer to 180°C, for 5 minutes.
2. In a mixing bowl, whisk together the eggs, milk, salt and pepper.
3. Stir in the diced vegetables, diced ham or bacon, and grated cheese.
4. Lightly spray the air fryer basket with cooking spray.
5. Pour the egg mixture into the basket and smooth out the surface.
6. Cook for 8-10 minutes or until the edges are set and the centre is cooked through.
7. Serve and enjoy!

Note: Feel free to add more vegetables or meat for extra flavour and protein.

# Breakfast Biscuit Bombs

**SERVES 4**

Brace yourselves for a breakfast explosion of flavours and goodness! Introducing the Breakfast Biscuit Bombs recipe for the air fryer. These little bombs are packed with all the breakfast favourites such as bacon, eggs, and cheese, wrapped in flaky and buttery biscuits, and then air-fried to golden perfection.

They are easy to make and perfect for a quick breakfast on the go, or a fun brunch option with friends and family. These Breakfast Biscuit Bombs are also great for meal prepping and can be stored in the fridge for up to 3 days or in the freezer for up to a month. So, let's roll up our sleeves and get ready to make these delicious breakfast bombs!

**NUTRITION PER SERVING:**
CALORIES: 470
FAT: 29G
CARBOHYDRATES: 36G
PROTEIN: 17G

PREPARATION TIME: 5 MINS
COOK TIME: 10 MINS

## INGREDIENTS:

- 8 large biscuits (such as Jus-Rol or Pillsbury)
- 8 slices of cooked bacon
- 8 eggs
- Salt and pepper, to taste
- Cooking spray

## INSTRUCTIONS:

1. Preheat your air fryer to 180°C, for 5 minutes.
2. Flatten each biscuit with a rolling pin until it is about 1/4 inch thick.
3. Place a slice of cooked bacon and an egg on top of each biscuit, then season with salt and pepper.
4. Carefully wrap the biscuit around the filling, making sure to seal the edges.
5. Place the biscuit bombs in the air fryer basket and lightly spray with cooking spray.
6. Cook for 8-10 minutes or until the biscuits are golden brown and the eggs are cooked to your liking.
7. Serve and enjoy!

# Quiche Lorraine

## SERVES 4

Quiche Lorraine is a classic French dish that is perfect for breakfast, brunch or lunch. This recipe is perfect for those who are looking for a delicious, easy and healthy meal to make in their air fryer. It's made with a buttery crust, eggs, bacon, cream, and cheese, making it a satisfying dish that is perfect for any time of the day.

**NUTRITION PER SERVING:**
CALORIES: 485
FAT: 42G
CARBOHYDRATES: 18G
PROTEIN: 12G

PREPARATION TIME: 5 MINS
COOK TIME: 25 MINS

## INGREDIENTS:

- 1 sheet of pre-made puff pastry
- 4 slices of bacon, diced
- 80g of heavy cream
- 3 eggs
- 80g of grated Gruyere cheese
- Salt and pepper, to taste

## INSTRUCTIONS:

1. Preheat your air fryer to 180°C.
2. Roll out the puff pastry sheet on a lightly all-purpose floured surface and press it into the bottom and up the sides of a quiche dish.
3. In a skillet, cook the bacon until crispy. Drain on paper towels.
4. In a mixing bowl, whisk together the eggs, cream, cheese, salt, and pepper.
5. Spread the bacon over the pastry crust.
6. Pour the egg mixture over the bacon.
7. Place the quiche dish in the air fryer basket.
8. Cook in the air fryer for 20-25 minutes or until the pastry is golden brown and the filling is set.
9. Remove from the air fryer and let it cool down for a few minutes before serving.

# Pumpkin French Toast

**SERVES 4**

This Pumpkin French Toast is a perfect dish for busy mornings when you need a quick and easy breakfast that will keep you full and energized. This recipe uses a mixture of pumpkin puree, eggs, milk, and spices to make a delicious and flavourful batter for the French toast. It's then air-fried to perfection, giving it a crispy texture and a delicious flavour. It's a perfect way to enjoy the flavours of fall in a breakfast dish.

**NUTRITION PER SERVING:**
CALORIES: 240
FAT: 7G
CARBOHYDRATES: 34G
PROTEIN: 11G

PREPARATION TIME: 5 MINS
COOK TIME: 10 MINS

## INGREDIENTS:

- ○ 3 eggs
- ○ 200ml of milk
- ○ 150ml of pumpkin puree
- ○ 1 teaspoon of pumpkin pie spice
- ○ 1/4 teaspoon of salt
- ○ 8 slices of bread (any kind you prefer)
- ○ Powdered sugar and maple syrup for serving (optional)

## INSTRUCTIONS:

1. Preheat your air fryer to 180°C.
2. In a mixing bowl, whisk together the eggs, milk, pumpkin puree, pumpkin pie spice, and salt.
3. Dip the slices of bread into the mixture, making sure they are well coated.
4. Place the slices of bread in the air fryer basket.
5. Cook in the air fryer for 5-7 minutes on each side or until golden brown and crispy.
6. Remove from the air fryer and let it cool down for a few minutes before serving.
7. Serve with powdered sugar and maple syrup on top (if desired).

# Baked Avocado Egg

Avocado toast is a classic breakfast staple, but have you ever tried baking an egg inside of an avocado? This recipe takes it to the next level by using an air fryer to give the avocado a crispy texture and the egg a perfect runny yolk. It's a delicious and healthy way to start your day, packed with healthy fats and protein.

**NUTRITION PER SERVING:**
CALORIES: 239
FAT: 21G
CARBOHYDRATES: 9G
PROTEIN: 5G

PREPARATION TIME: 5 MINS
COOK TIME: 10 MINS

## INGREDIENTS:

- 1 avocado
- 1 egg
- Salt and pepper, to taste
- Optional: 1 tablespoon grated Parmesan cheese or any cheese of your choice

## INSTRUCTIONS:

1. Preheat your air fryer to 180°C.
2. Slice the avocado in half and remove the pit.
3. Crack an egg into the hole left by the pit, being careful not to break the yolk.
4. Season the egg with salt and pepper, and add cheese on top (if desired)
5. Place the avocado halves in the air fryer basket and cook for 8-10 minutes, or until the egg is cooked to your liking.
6. Remove from the air fryer and let it cool down for a few minutes before serving.

# Breakfast Puffed Egg Tarts

## SERVES 4

Are you ready for a breakfast treat that is both delicious and healthy? Introducing our Breakfast Puffed Egg Tarts recipe for the air fryer. This recipe is a great way to start your day off right, with a nutritious and delicious breakfast option. These egg tarts are made with a flaky crust, a creamy egg filling, and a sprinkle of cheese. Cooked in the air fryer, they puff up beautifully and have a crispy crust while the filling stays soft and creamy.

This recipe is perfect for meal prepping and can be stored in the fridge for up to 3 days or in the freezer for up to a month. So, let's preheat our air fryers and make these delicious breakfast tarts!

**NUTRITION PER SERVING:**
CALORIES: 191
FAT: 14G
CARBOHYDRATES: 12G
PROTEIN: 6G

PREPARATION TIME: 5 MINS
COOK TIME: 10 MINS

## INGREDIENTS:

- 1 sheet of puff pastry
- 2 large eggs
- 2 tablespoons of milk
- 2 tablespoons of grated cheese
- Salt and pepper, to taste

## INSTRUCTIONS:

1. Preheat your air fryer to 180°C.
2. Roll out the puff pastry sheet on a lightly all-purpose floured surface to about 0.5cm thickness.
3. Cut the pastry sheet into 4 squares.
4. In a mixing bowl, whisk together the eggs, milk, cheese, salt, and pepper.
5. Place the squares of pastry in the air fryer basket and spoon the egg mixture into each square.
6. Cook in the air fryer for 8-10 minutes, or until the pastry is puffed and golden brown.
7. Remove from the air fryer and let it cool down for a few minutes before serving.

# Full English Breakfast

## SERVES 4

Introducing our full English breakfast recipe for the air fryer. This recipe is the perfect way to enjoy a classic and hearty breakfast without the hassle of stovetop cooking. The air fryer gives the bacon, sausages, and tomatoes a crispy texture while keeping the eggs and mushrooms perfectly cooked.

Served with toast and baked beans, this full English breakfast is perfect for weekend brunch or a special occasion breakfast. It's also a great way to meal prep for the week ahead. So, let's gather our ingredients and cook up a delicious and satisfying full English breakfast in the air fryer.

**NUTRITION PER SERVING:**
CALORIES: 590
FAT: 45G
CARBOHYDRATES: 6G
PROTEIN: 30G

PREPARATION TIME: 10 MINS
COOK TIME: 20 MINS

## INGREDIENTS:

- ○ 4 large eggs
- ○ 4 slices of bacon
- ○ 4 sausages
- ○ 4 mushrooms, sliced
- ○ 4 tomatoes, halved
- ○ Salt and pepper, to taste
- ○ 2 tablespoons of olive oil

## INSTRUCTIONS:

1. Preheat the air fryer to 200°C.
2. Place the sausages and bacon in the air fryer basket and cook for 12-15 minutes or until cooked through and crispy.
3. Remove the sausages and bacon from the air fryer and set aside.
4. Add the mushrooms and tomatoes to the air fryer basket and drizzle with olive oil. Season with salt and pepper.
5. Cook for 8-10 minutes or until the mushrooms and tomatoes are tender.
6. Remove the mushrooms and tomatoes from the air fryer and set aside.
7. Crack the eggs into the air fryer basket and cook for 3-5 minutes or until the whites are set and the yolks are cooked to your desired level.
8. Serve all ingredients on a plate and enjoy!

# Breakfast Burrito

Breakfast burritos are a delicious and satisfying way to start your day. They are packed with protein, fibre, and flavour, making them a perfect choice for busy mornings when you need a quick and easy breakfast that will keep you full and energized. This recipe uses the air fryer to give the tortillas a crispy texture, while the filling is made with black beans, corn, bell pepper, onion, and cumin, all wrapped in a warm whole wheat tortilla and topped with shredded cheese. Serve it with salsa and sour cream to give it an extra kick of flavour. This recipe is easy to make, delicious and perfect for a quick breakfast on the go.

**NUTRITION PER SERVING:**
CALORIES: 456
FAT: 18G
CARBOHYDRATES: 51G
PROTEIN: 22G

PREPARATION TIME: 5 MINS
COOK TIME: 10 MINS

## INGREDIENTS:

- 1 can black beans, rinsed and drained (240g)
- 50g frozen corn
- 25g diced red bell pepper
- 25g diced onion
- 1/4 teaspoon ground cumin
- Salt and pepper, to taste
- 4 large eggs
- 4 (20cm) whole wheat tortillas
- 50g shredded cheddar cheese
- Salsa and sour cream, for serving (optional)

## INSTRUCTIONS:

1. Preheat your air fryer to 200C.
2. In a mixing bowl, combine the black beans, corn, bell pepper, onion, cumin, salt, and pepper.
3. Crack the eggs into a separate bowl and beat them with a fork.
4. Place a tortilla on a plate and spoon about 60g of the bean mixture in the centre of the tortilla.
5. Add a pinch of cheese on top of the bean mixture.
6. Carefully roll up the tortilla, tucking in the sides as you go. Repeat with the remaining tortillas and filling.
7. Place the rolled-up tortillas in the air fryer basket and lightly coat them with cooking spray.
8. Air fry for 7-8 minutes, or until the tortillas are crispy and the cheese is melted.
9. Serve with salsa and sour cream, if desired.

# Cheese & Onion Omelette

## SERVES 4

Here is a great balanced breakfast dish, the classic omelette, with cheese and onions. The cheese adds a creamy and decadent touch, while the onions add a flavourful to`uch. You can add or replace some ingredients like mushrooms, bell peppers, or spinach if you like. It's a good source of protein, vitamins, and minerals and it's also a good way to start your day with a healthy and satisfying breakfast.

**NUTRITION PER SERVING:**
CALORIES: 150
FAT: 11G
CARBOHYDRATES: 2G
PROTEIN: 10G

PREPARATION TIME: 5 MINS
COOK TIME: 10 MINS

## INGREDIENTS:

- 4 large eggs
- 40g of diced onions
- 40g of shredded cheese (cheddar, mozzarella or gouda)
- Salt and pepper, to taste
- 1 tablespoon of olive oil

## INSTRUCTIONS:

1. In a small bowl, beat the eggs, diced onions, shredded cheese, salt and pepper together.
2. Preheat the air fryer to 200°C.
3. Grease the air fryer basket with olive oil.
4. Pour the egg mixture into the air fryer basket.
5. Cook for 8-10 minutes or until the eggs are set and golden brown.
6. Carefully remove the omelette from the air fryer and fold it in half.
7. Serve and enjoy!

# Lamb Bhuna with Keema Rice

## SERVES 4

Get ready for a culinary adventure with this delicious Lamb Bhuna with Keema Rice recipe for the air fryer! This recipe is a fusion of traditional Indian flavours with a modern twist of air fryer cooking. The lamb is marinated in a mouth watering bhuna sauce and then air-fried until tender and succulent, while the keema rice is cooked with aromatic spices and peas. This recipe is sure to delight your taste buds and take you on a flavourful journey. It's perfect for a special occasion or a fun weekend dinner. So, let's put on our chef hats and get ready to cook up a storm with this Lamb Bhuna with Keema Rice recipe for the air fryer!

### NUTRITION PER SERVING:
CALORIES: 640
FAT: 30G
CARBOHYDRATES: 40G
PROTEIN: 40G

PREPARATION TIME: 10 MINS
COOK TIME: 45 MINS

## INGREDIENTS:

- 500g lamb, cut into bite-sized pieces
- 2 tablespoons vegetable oil
- 2 onions, finely chopped
- 2 cloves of garlic, minced
- 2 tablespoons ginger paste
- 2 tablespoons tomato puree
- 2 tablespoons ground cumin
- 2 tablespoons ground coriander
- 2 tablespoons garam masala
- 1 tablespoon ground turmeric
- Salt and pepper, to taste
- 100g minced lamb
- 100g Basmati rice
- 200ml water
- Cooking spray

## INSTRUCTIONS:

1. Preheat your air fryer to 180°C, for 5 minutes.
2. In the air fryer basket, heat the oil and add the onions, garlic, ginger paste and cook for 2-3 minutes until softened.
3. Add the tomato puree, cumin, coriander, garam masala, turmeric, salt and pepper, and cook for 2 minutes.
4. Add the lamb and cook for 10-15 minutes or until the lamb is browned and tender.
5. Add the minced lamb and cook for another 5 minutes.
6. In a separate container, mix the washed rice and water and place it on top of the lamb mixture.
7. Cook for 25-30 minutes or until the lamb is cooked through and the rice is tender.
8. Serve and enjoy!

# Recipes – Dinner

# Salt and Pepper Chicken Wings with Rice and Wedges

## SERVES 4

Introducing Salt and Pepper Chicken Wings with Rice and wedges in an air fryer. A scrumptious and simple way to enjoy a delicious and satisfying meal. Made with crispy chicken wings, fluffy rice and wedges, this recipe is perfect for a week-night dinner or a special occasion. Plus, it's cooked all in one place, your trusty air fryer, so you can spend less time in the kitchen and more time with your loved ones.

**NUTRITION PER SERVING:**
CALORIES: 750
FAT: 28G
CARBOHYDRATES: 48G
PROTEIN: 39G

PREPARATION TIME: 10 MINS
COOK TIME: 20 MINS

## INGREDIENTS:

- O 500g chicken wings
- O 2 tablespoons salt
- O 2 tablespoons black pepper
- O 2 tablespoons vegetable oil
- O 100g basmati rice
- O 200ml water
- O 2 large potatoes, cut into wedges
- O Cooking spray

## INSTRUCTIONS:

1. Preheat your air fryer to 180°C, for 5 minutes.
2. In a mixing bowl, combine the chicken wings, salt, pepper and oil, toss to coat.
3. Place the chicken wings in the air fryer basket and cook for 15-20 minutes or until golden brown and crispy.
4. In a separate container, mix the washed rice and water, and place it on top of the chicken wings.
5. Place the potato wedges in a separate container and spray with oil, add salt and pepper to taste.
6. Place the container with potatoes in the air fryer and cook for 15-20 minutes or until golden brown and crispy.
7. Serve and enjoy!

# Home-made Lasagne with Greens

## SERVES 4

This recipe for Home-made Lasagne with Greens in an air fryer is a delicious and easy way to enjoy the classic Italian dish. Made with a rich and flavourful meat sauce, tender pasta layers, and a variety of greens, this recipe is perfect for a week-night dinner or a special occasion. Plus, it's cooked all in one place, your trusty air fryer, so you can spend less time in the kitchen and more time with your loved ones.

**NUTRITION PER SERVING:**
CALORIES: 640
FAT: 22G
CARBOHYDRATES: 44G
PROTEIN: 26G

PREPARATION TIME: 10 MINS
COOK TIME: 30 MINS

## INGREDIENTS:

- ○ 500g ground beef
- ○ 1 onion, diced
- ○ 2 cloves of garlic, minced
- ○ 500ml of marinara sauce
- ○ 500g of chopped spinach, kale or other greens
- ○ 8-10 lasagne noodles, cooked according to package instructions
- ○ 500g of ricotta cheese
- ○ 250g of grated mozzarella cheese
- ○ Salt and pepper, to taste
- ○ Cooking spray

## INSTRUCTIONS:

1. Preheat your air fryer to 180°C, for 5 minutes.
2. In a pan, brown the beef over medium heat and season with salt and pepper.
3. Add the onions and garlic and cook for 2-3 minutes.
4. Stir in the marinara sauce and greens, cook until the greens are wilted.
5. In a mixing bowl, combine the ricotta cheese with salt and pepper.
6. In a 9x9 inch (23x23 cm) baking dish that fits in your air fryer, layer the lasagne noodles, meat, sauce, ricotta mixture, and mozzarella cheese.
7. Lightly coat the top of the lasagna with cooking spray.
8. Cook in the air fryer for 20-25 minutes or until the cheese is melted and bubbly.
9. Serve and enjoy!

# Full English Roast Dinner

### SERVES 4

The Full English Roast Dinner in an air fryer is a great dish to make for family gatherings. Made with tender roast beef, crispy roast potatoes, and a variety of other traditional sides, this recipe is perfect for a special occasion or a Sunday dinner. Plus, it's cooked all in one place, your trusty air fryer, so you can spend less time in the kitchen and more time with your loved ones.

**NUTRITION PER SERVING:**
CALORIES: 600
FAT: 25G
CARBOHYDRATES: 35G
PROTEIN: 42G

PREPARATION TIME: 10 MINS
COOK TIME: 30 MINS

## INGREDIENTS:

- 1kg beef roast
- 1 tablespoon salt
- 1 tablespoon pepper
- 1 tablespoon garlic powder
- 1 tablespoon dried thyme
- 2 tablespoons vegetable oil
- 1 kg potatoes, peeled and cut into wedges
- 1 onion, diced
- 2 cloves of garlic, minced
- 500g of frozen peas
- 8-10 carrots, peeled and cut into chunks
- Cooking spray

## INSTRUCTIONS:

1. Preheat your air fryer to 180°C, for 5 minutes.
2. In a mixing bowl, combine the salt, pepper, garlic powder, thyme, and oil. Rub the mixture on the roast beef.
3. Place the roast beef in the air fryer basket and cook for 25-30 minutes or until the desired cooking is achieved.
4. In a separate container, toss the potatoes, onion and garlic with some oil, salt and pepper. Place the container in the air fryer and cook for 20-25 minutes or until golden brown and crispy.
5. In a separate container, place the frozen peas and carrots and cook for 10-15 minutes or until tender.
6. Serve and enjoy!

Also, you may want to add some more vegetables or sides to your roast dinner, such as gravy, stuffing, or Yorkshire pudding.

# Cajun Salmon with New Potatoes

**SERVES 4**

This recipe for Cajun Salmon with New Potatoes in an air fryer is a simple and satisfying way to enjoy a healthy and flavourful meal. Made with wild caught salmon fillets, seasoned with a spicy Cajun blend, and paired with new potatoes, this recipe is perfect for a week-night dinner or a special occasion. Plus, it's cooked all in one place, your trusty air fryer, so you can spend less time in the kitchen and more time with your loved ones.

**NUTRITION PER SERVING:**
CALORIES: 620
FAT: 20G
CARBOHYDRATES: 46G
PROTEIN: 33G

PREPARATION TIME: 10 MINS
COOK TIME: 40 MINS

## INGREDIENTS:

- 4 salmon fillets, skin on
- 2 tablespoons cajun seasoning
- 1 tablespoon olive oil
- 1 kg new potatoes, washed and cut in half
- Salt and pepper, to taste
- Cooking spray

## INSTRUCTIONS:

1. Preheat your air fryer to 180°C, for 5 minutes.
2. In a mixing bowl, combine the Cajun seasoning and olive oil. Rub the mixture on the salmon fillets.
3. Place the salmon fillets in the air fryer basket, skin side down and cook for 10-12 minutes or until the salmon is cooked through.
4. In a separate container, toss the new potatoes with some oil, salt and pepper. Place the container in the air fryer and cook for 20-25 minutes or until tender.
5. Serve and enjoy!

# Beef Stroganoff with Boiled Rice

## SERVES 4

Beef Stroganoff with Boiled Rice in an air fryer is a delightful way to enjoy a classic Russian dish. Made with tender beef, mushrooms, and a rich and creamy sauce, this recipe is perfect for a week-night dinner or a special occasion. Plus, it's cooked all in one place, your trusty air fryer, so you can spend less time in the kitchen and more time with your loved ones.

**NUTRITION PER SERVING:**
CALORIES: 780
FAT: 32G
CARBOHYDRATES: 53G
PROTEIN: 38G

PREPARATION TIME: 10 MINS
COOK TIME: 25 MINS

## INGREDIENTS:

- ○ 500g beef sirloin or beef tenderloin, cut into thin strips
- ○ 1 onion, diced
- ○ 2 cloves of garlic, minced
- ○ 200g mushrooms, sliced
- ○ 2 tablespoons all-purpose flour
- ○ 500ml of beef broth
- ○ 250ml of sour cream
- ○ 1 tablespoon Dijon mustard
- ○ Salt and pepper, to taste
- ○ 100g basmati rice
- ○ 200ml water

## INSTRUCTIONS:

1. Preheat your air fryer to 180°C, for 5 minutes.
2. In a pan, brown the beef over medium heat and season with salt and pepper.
3. Add the onions, garlic, mushrooms, all-purpose flour and stir it constantly, cook for 2-3 minutes.
4. Stir in the beef broth and bring to a boil.
5. Reduce the heat and stir in the sour cream and Dijon mustard.
6. In a separate container, mix the washed rice and water, and place it on top of the beef mixture.
7. Place the container in the air fryer and cook for 20-25 minutes or until the rice is tender.
8. Serve and enjoy!

# Crispy Duck and Pancakes with Hoisin Sauce

## SERVES 4

This recipe for Crispy Duck and Pancakes with Hoisin Sauce in an air fryer is a delicious and easy way to enjoy the classic Chinese dish. Made with crispy duck and fluffy pancakes, paired with a sweet and savoury hoisin sauce, this recipe is perfect for a special occasion or a comforting week-night dinner. Plus, it's cooked all in one place, your trusty air fryer, so you can spend less time in the kitchen and more time with your loved ones.

**NUTRITION PER SERVING:**
CALORIES: 850
FAT: 44G
CARBOHYDRATES: 49G
PROTEIN: 21G

PREPARATION TIME: 1 HOUR
COOK TIME: 35 MINS

## INGREDIENTS:

- 1 whole duck, cleaned and prepared for roasting
- 2 tablespoons hoisin sauce
- 2 tablespoons honey
- 1 tablespoon soy sauce
- 1 tablespoon rice vinegar
- 1 tablespoon Chinese five spice powder
- 1/2 tablespoon salt
- 250g of all-purpose flour
- 250ml of water
- 500ml of vegetable oil
- Cooking spray

## INSTRUCTIONS:

1. Preheat your air fryer to 180°C, for 5 minutes.
2. In a mixing bowl, combine the hoisin sauce, honey, soy sauce, rice vinegar, Chinese five spice powder, and salt. Rub the mixture on the duck and set aside to marinate for at least 1 hour.
3. Cover the duck in cooking oil, before placing the duck in the air fryer basket, skin side down and cook for 20-25 minutes or until the skin is brown and crispy, and the duck is cooked through.
4. Cover the duck in cooking oil again, before placing the duck in the air fryer for a further 5-7 minutes, or until the batter is golden brown and crispy.
5. Serve with the pancakes and hoisin sauce and enjoy!

# Shrimp La Bang Bang

## SERVES 4

This recipe for Bang Bang Shrimp in an air fryer is a scrumptious and simple way to enjoy the classic dish. Made with crispy breaded shrimp and coated in a sweet and spicy sauce, this recipe is perfect for a week-night dinner or a special occasion. Plus, it's cooked all in one place, your trusty air fryer, so you can spend less time in the kitchen and more time with your loved ones.

**NUTRITION PER SERVING:**
CALORIES: 730
FAT: 34G
CARBOHYDRATES: 41G
PROTEIN: 30G

PREPARATION TIME: 10 MINS
COOK TIME: 15 MINS

## INGREDIENTS:

- 450g of raw shrimp, peeled and deveined
- 125g of all-purpose flour
- 1 tablespoon salt
- 1 tablespoon pepper
- 1 tablespoon garlic powder
- 2 eggs, beaten
- 125g of panko breadcrumbs
- 125ml of mayonnaise
- 2 tablespoons of sweet chilli sauce
- 2 tablespoons of honey
- 1 tablespoon of rice vinegar
- 1 tablespoon of sriracha sauce
- Cooking spray

## INSTRUCTIONS:

1. Preheat your air fryer to 180°C, for 5 minutes.
2. In a mixing bowl, combine the all-purpose flour, salt, pepper and garlic powder.
3. In another bowl, beat the eggs.
4. In a third bowl, add the panko breadcrumbs.
5. Dip the shrimp in the all-purpose flour mixture, then the beaten eggs, and finally coat it in the panko breadcrumbs.
6. Place the shrimp in the air fryer basket and cook for 10-12 minutes or until golden brown and crispy.
7. In a separate mixing bowl, combine mayonnaise, sweet chilli sauce, honey, rice vinegar, and sriracha sauce.
8. Once the shrimp is done, toss it in the sauce and cook for an additional 1-2 minutes or until the sauce is heated through.
9. Serve and enjoy!

# Chicken Parmesan

## SERVES 4

Introducing a new way to enjoy classic comfort food - air fryer Chicken Parmesan! This recipe is a healthier alternative to the traditional deep-fried version, and it's just as delicious. The air fryer gives the chicken a crispy crust while keeping it juicy on the inside. The addition of marinara sauce and mozzarella cheese makes for a mouthwatering and satisfying dinner. Give it a try tonight and enjoy the taste without the guilt!

### NUTRITION PER SERVING:
CALORIES: 680
FAT: 21G
CARBOHYDRATES: 42G
PROTEIN: 48G

PREPARATION TIME: 10 MINS
COOK TIME: 20 MINS

## INGREDIENTS:

- ○ 4 boneless, skinless chicken breasts (about 500g)
- ○ 125g all-purpose flour
- ○ 2 eggs, beaten
- ○ 100g breadcrumbs
- ○ 25g grated Parmesan cheese
- ○ 5g dried basil
- ○ 2.5g garlic powder
- ○ Salt and pepper to taste
- ○ 250g marinara sauce
- ○ 100g shredded mozzarella cheese

## INSTRUCTIONS:

1. Preheat your air fryer to 200°C.
2. In a shallow dish, mix together the all-purpose flour, basil, garlic powder, salt and pepper.
3. In another shallow dish, beat the eggs.
4. In a third shallow dish, mix together the breadcrumbs and grated Parmesan.
5. Dip each chicken breast in the all-purpose flour mixture, then the egg mixture, and finally the breadcrumb mixture.
6. Place the chicken in the air fryer and cook for 12-15 minutes.
7. Remove the chicken from the air fryer and top with marinara sauce and shredded mozzarella cheese.
8. Place the chicken back in the air fryer and cook for an additional 3-5 minutes, until the cheese is melted and bubbly.
9. Serve with a side of pasta or a green salad, and enjoy your delicious and healthier version!

# Salsa Chicken Taquitos

## SERVES 4

Time for a fiesta in your mouth with these delicious air fryer Salsa Chicken Taquitos! These little rolled up treats are packed with flavour and made healthier by using an air fryer. These air fryer Salsa Chicken Taquitos are perfect for game night with friends or as a party appetizer. Add them to your next fiesta menu and watch them disappear faster than you can say "ole!"

**NUTRITION PER SERVING:**
CALORIES: 667
FAT: 15G
CARBOHYDRATES: 32G
PROTEIN: 42G

PREPARATION TIME: 10 MINS
COOK TIME: 20 MINS

## INGREDIENTS:

- 500g boneless, skinless chicken breast
- 120g salsa
- 30g diced onion
- 30g diced bell pepper
- 30g diced jalapeño (optional)
- 5g chilli powder
- 5g cumin
- Salt and pepper, to taste
- 200g all-purpose flour tortillas
- Cooking spray

## INSTRUCTIONS:

1. Preheat your air fryer to 200°C.
2. In a medium bowl, mix together the 500g chicken, 120g salsa, 30g onion, 30g bell pepper, 30g jalapeño (if using), 5g chilli powder, 5g cumin, salt, and pepper.
3. Place a heaping tablespoon (about 30g) of the chicken mixture onto the centre of each 200g tortilla. Roll the tortilla tightly around the filling and secure the edges with toothpicks.
4. Lightly coat the taquitos with cooking spray.
5. Place the taquitos in the air fryer basket. Cook for 20 minutes, or until golden brown and crispy.
6. Remove the taquitos from the air fryer and let them cool for a few minutes before removing the toothpicks.
7. Serve with your favourite dipping sauce and enjoy!

# BBQ Baby Back Ribs

**SERVES 4**

Fire up your taste buds with this mouthwatering BBQ Baby Back Ribs recipe for the air fryer! This recipe is the perfect way to enjoy fall-off-the-bone ribs without the hassle of grilling or smoking. The ribs are marinated in a home-made BBQ sauce and then air-fried to perfection. The result is a tender and succulent meat with a crispy and flavourful crust.

This recipe is perfect for a summer cook-out, a game day feast or any occasion that calls for some finger-licking good ribs. It's also great for meal prepping and can be stored in the fridge for up to 3 days or in the freezer for up to a month. So, let's get our aprons on and get ready to cook up some delicious BBQ Baby Back Ribs in the air fryer!

**NUTRITION PER SERVING:**
CALORIES: 551
FAT: 35G
CARBOHYDRATES: 13G
PROTEIN: 42G

PREPARATION TIME: 10 MINS
COOK TIME: 40 MINS

## INGREDIENTS:

- ○ 1 kg baby back ribs
- ○ 2 tablespoons paprika
- ○ 2 tablespoons brown sugar
- ○ 1 tablespoon garlic powder
- ○ 1 tablespoon onion powder
- ○ 1 tablespoon salt
- ○ 1 tablespoon black pepper
- ○ 100ml BBQ sauce

## INSTRUCTIONS:

1. Preheat your air fryer to 180°C, for 5 minutes.
2. In a small bowl, mix together the paprika, brown sugar, garlic powder, onion powder, salt, and black pepper.
3. Rub the spice mixture all over the ribs, making sure to coat evenly.
4. Place the ribs in the air fryer and cook for 25 minutes.
5. Brush the BBQ sauce onto the ribs and cook for an additional 10 minutes.
6. Remove from the air fryer and let the ribs rest for 5 minutes before cutting and serving.
7. Serve with a side of your choice and enjoy the finger-licking goodness!

# Turkey Fajitas

**SERVES 4**

Get ready to spice up your dinner routine with this delicious Turkey Fajitas recipe for the air fryer! This recipe is a fun and healthy twist on the traditional beef fajitas. The turkey is marinated in a flavourful blend of spices and then air-fried to perfection. Served with sautéed peppers and onions and wrapped in warm tortillas, these fajitas are sure to be a hit with the whole family.

This recipe is perfect for a week-night dinner or a fun and casual get-together with friends. It's also great for meal prepping and can be stored in the fridge for up to 3 days or in the freezer for up to a month. So, let's gather our ingredients, fire up our air fryers and get ready for a fiesta of flavours with these Turkey Fajitas!

**NUTRITION PER SERVING:**
CALORIE: 343
FAT: 13G
CARBOHYDRATES: 27G
PROTEIN: 29G

PREPARATION TIME: 10 MINS
COOK TIME: 20 MINS

## INGREDIENTS:

- 500g turkey breast, sliced into thin strips
- 1 red bell pepper, sliced
- 1 green bell pepper, sliced
- 1 yellow onion, sliced
- 2 cloves of garlic, minced
- 2 tablespoons olive oil
- 2 teaspoons chili powder
- 1 teaspoon ground cumin
- 1 teaspoon smoked paprika
- 1/2 teaspoon salt
- 1/4 teaspoon black pepper
- 1/4 teaspoon cayenne pepper (optional)
- 8 tortillas
- Optional toppings: shredded cheese, sour cream, avocado, cilantro

1. Preheat your air fryer to 180°C, for 5 minutes.
2. In a large bowl, mix together the turkey strips, sliced bell peppers, sliced onion, minced garlic, olive oil, chili powder, ground cumin, smoked paprika, salt, black pepper, and cayenne pepper (if using).
3. Place the turkey and vegetables in the air fryer basket and cook for 15-20 minutes, or until the turkey is cooked through and the vegetables are tender.
4. Remove the turkey and vegetables from the air fryer and place them in a serving dish.
5. Serve the turkey and vegetables on warm all-purpose flour tortillas and toppings of your choice.
6. Enjoy your delicious and healthy turkey fajitas!

# Katsu Chicken

**SERVES 4**

This recipe is a fun and healthy twist on the traditional deep-fried Katsu Chicken, which originated in Japan. The chicken is coated in a crispy panko breadcrumb crust and then air-fried to perfection, resulting in a crispy exterior and juicy interior. Served with a side of rice and a tangy tonkatsu sauce, this dish is sure to transport your taste buds straight to Japan. It's perfect for a week-night dinner or a fun and casual get-together with friends. So, let's gather our ingredients, fire up our air fryers and get ready for a delicious and cultural culinary experience with this Katsu Chicken air fryer recipe!

**NUTRITION PER SERVING:**
CALORIE: 722
FAT: 18G
CARBOHYDRATES: 57G
PROTEIN: 54G

PREPARATION TIME: 10 MINS
COOK TIME: 20 MINS

## INGREDIENTS:

- 4 boneless, skinless chicken breasts (about 600g)
- 60g all-purpose flour
- 2 eggs, beaten
- 200g panko bread crumbs
- Salt and pepper to taste

### For the Katsu sauce:

- 60ml soy sauce
- 2 tablespoons Worcestershire sauce
- 1 tablespoon sugar
- 1 tablespoon ketchup
- 1 teaspoon rice vinegar
- 1/2 teaspoon garlic powder
- 1/4 teaspoon onion powder
- 1/4 teaspoon mustard powder

## INSTRUCTIONS:

1. Preheat your air fryer to 180°C, for 5 minutes.
2. In a shallow dish, combine the all-purpose flour and a pinch of salt and pepper. In a separate shallow dish, beat the eggs. In a third shallow dish, add the panko bread crumbs.
3. Dip each chicken breast in the all-purpose flour mixture, then the eggs, and then coat with the bread crumbs.
4. Place the chicken in the air fryer basket and cook for 15-20 minutes, or until the chicken is cooked through and golden brown.
5. Meanwhile, in a small saucepan over medium heat, whisk together all of the katsu sauce ingredients. Bring to a simmer and cook for 2-3 minutes, or until the sauce has thickened.
6. Once chicken is cooked, remove from the air fryer and serve with the katsu sauce.
7. Enjoy your crispy, juicy and delicious chicken katsu with a tangy and savoury katsu sauce.

# Sweet Potato Fries

Fancy some crispy and delicious sweet potato fries but don't want the added guilt of deep-frying? This recipe for air fryer sweet potato fries is quick, easy, and compliment many different dishes! Not only is it simple to make, but it's also a healthier alternative to traditional deep-frying. So grab your apron and let's get to making some delicious fries!

**NUTRITION PER SERVING:**
CALORIE: 256
FAT: 6G
CARBOHYDRATES: 24G
PROTEIN: 2G

PREPARATION TIME: 10 MINS
COOK TIME: 15 MINS

## INGREDIENTS:

- 2 medium sweet potatoes (about 400g), peeled and cut into fries
- 2 tablespoons olive oil
- 1 teaspoon salt
- 1/2 teaspoon black pepper
- 1/4 teaspoon garlic powder (optional)

## INSTRUCTIONS:

1. Preheat your air fryer to 180°C, for 5 minutes.
2. In a large bowl, toss the sweet potato fries with olive oil, salt, pepper, and garlic powder (if using).
3. Place the sweet potatoes in the air fryer basket and cook for 12-15 minutes, or until the fries are crispy and golden brown.
4. Remove the fries from the air fryer and serve immediately.
5. Enjoy your crispy and delicious sweet potato fries!

# Home-made Pizza

It's Pizza Night but you don't want to wait for delivery or have the added guilt of eating out? Look no further than this recipe for air fryer home-made pizza! Not only is it easy to make, but it also allows you to customize it with your favourite toppings. So grab your apron and let's get cooking!

**NUTRITION PER SERVING:**
CALORIE: 240
FAT: 7G
CARBOHYDRATES: 32G
PROTEIN: 10G

PREPARATION TIME: 10 MINS
COOK TIME: 10 MINS

## INGREDIENTS:

- 1 pre-made pizza crust (about 250g)
- 60ml tomato sauce
- 30g shredded mozzarella cheese
- 2 tablespoons grated Parmesan cheese
- 1/4 teaspoon Italian seasoning
- Toppings of your choice (such as pepperoni, mushrooms, onions, bell peppers, etc.)

## INSTRUCTIONS:

1. Preheat the air fryer to 180°C, for 5 minutes.
2. Place the pizza crust in the air fryer and cook for 2-3 minutes, or until it starts to puff up.
3. Remove the crust from the air fryer and spread the tomato sauce on top, leaving a 1/2-inch border around the edges.
4. Sprinkle the mozzarella and Parmesan cheese on top of the sauce.
5. Add your desired toppings and sprinkle with Italian seasoning.
6. Place the pizza back in the air fryer and cook for 8-10 minutes, or until the cheese is melted and the crust is golden brown.
7. Remove the pizza from the air fryer and let it cool for a few minutes before slicing and serving.
8. Enjoy your home-made and delicious pizza!

# Spicy Chicken Jerky

### SERVES 4

Craving something spicy and savoury? Look no further than this recipe for air fryer spicy chicken jerky! Not only is it easy to make, but it's also a healthier alternative to store-bought jerky. Perfect for a snack or a road trip, it will give you the kick you need. So grab your apron and let's get to making some delicious jerky!

**NUTRITION PER SERVING:**
CALORIE: 208
FAT: 4G
CARBOHYDRATES: 11G
PROTEIN: 31G

PREPARATION TIME: 2 HOURS
COOK TIME: 20 MINS

## INGREDIENTS:

- 500g boneless, skinless chicken breast, cut into thin strips
- 2 tablespoons soy sauce
- 2 tablespoons Worcestershire sauce
- 2 tablespoons honey
- 2 teaspoons sriracha sauce
- 1 teaspoon garlic powder
- 1/2 teaspoon onion powder
- 1/2 teaspoon smoked paprika
- 1/4 teaspoon black pepper

**INSTRUCTIONS:**

1. Preheat the air fryer to 180°C, for 5 minutes.
2. In a small bowl, whisk together soy sauce, Worcestershire sauce, honey, sriracha sauce, garlic powder, onion powder, smoked paprika, and black pepper.
3. Place the chicken strips in a large resealable bag or bowl and pour the marinade over the top. Toss to coat the chicken evenly.
4. Refrigerate for at least 2 hours or overnight.
5. Place chicken strips in the air fryer basket and cook for 15-20 minutes, or until the chicken is cooked through and crispy.
6. Remove the chicken from the air fryer and let it cool for a few minutes before serving
7. Enjoy your delicious and spicy chicken jerky!

# Jacket Potato with Salad

Looking for a comforting and healthy meal? Try this classic recipe for air fryer baked potatoes with salad. This recipe is easy to make, and it's a perfect balance of healthy carbs and greens. It's also a great way to use up any leftover ingredients you might have in your fridge. So grab your apron and let's get to making some delicious potatoes!

**NUTRITION PER SERVING:**
CALORIE: 285
FAT: 12G
CARBOHYDRATES: 41G
PROTEIN: 7G

PREPARATION TIME: 10 MINS
COOK TIME: 40 MINS

## INGREDIENTS:

- ○ 4 medium potatoes (about 800g)
- ○ 2 tablespoons olive oil
- ○ Salt and pepper to taste
- ○ 200g mixed greens
- ○ 30g crumbled feta cheese
- ○ 2 tablespoons balsamic vinaigrette
- ○ 30g chopped cherry tomatoes
- ○ 2 tablespoons chopped red onions
- ○ 2 tablespoons chopped cucumber
- ○ 2 tablespoons chopped bell pepper

## INSTRUCTIONS:

1. Preheat the air fryer to 180°C, for 5 minutes.
2. Rinse the potatoes and pat dry. Prick the potatoes with a fork several times.
3. Brush the potatoes with olive oil and season with salt and pepper.
4. Place the potatoes in the air fryer basket and cook for 30-40 minutes, or until the potatoes are tender and fully cooked.
5. Remove the potatoes from the air fryer and let them cool for a few minutes.
6. While the potatoes are cooling, in a large bowl, combine the mixed greens, feta cheese, balsamic vinaigrette, cherry tomatoes, red onions, cucumber, and bell pepper.
7. Cut the potatoes in half and fluff the insides with a fork. Top with the salad mixture.
8. Enjoy your comforting and healthy air fryer baked potatoes with salad!

# Rotisserie Chicken

## SERVES 4

Introducing the crispy, juicy, and flavourful recipe for Rotisserie-style air fryer Chicken! This recipe will take your taste buds on a wild ride and leave you feeling satisfied and full of energy. Not only is this recipe delicious, but it's also a healthier alternative to traditional rotisserie chicken, and you can add many different sides or appetisers from this cookbook such as stuffed mushrooms or vegetables to create a hearty dish.

**NUTRITION PER SERVING:**
CALORIES: 170
FAT: 9G
CARBOHYDRATES: 0G
PROTEIN: 22G

PREPARATION TIME: 10 MINS
COOK TIME: 1 HOUR 20 MINS

## INGREDIENTS:

- 1 whole chicken (about 1.5 kg)
- 2 tablespoons olive oil
- 1 tablespoon salt
- 1 tablespoon black pepper
- 1 tablespoon paprika
- 1 tablespoon garlic powder
- 1 tablespoon onion powder

## INSTRUCTIONS:

1. Preheat the air fryer to 180°C, for 5 minutes.
2. In a small bowl, mix together the olive oil, salt, pepper, paprika, garlic powder, and onion powder to make a rub.
3. Pat the chicken dry with paper towels and then rub the seasoning mixture all over the chicken, making sure to get it in all the nooks and crannies.
4. Place the seasoned chicken in the air fryer basket and cook for about 1 hour and 15 minutes or until cooked through.
5. Once the chicken is cooked through, let it rest for a few minutes before carving and serving.
6. Enjoy your delicious and healthy rotisserie-style air fryer chicken!

# Meatloaf

## SERVES 4

Meatloaf is a classic comfort food that can be enjoyed any time of the year, but why spend hours in the kitchen when you can have it ready in no time with your trusty air fryer? This recipe is sure to be a hit with your family and friends!

**NUTRITION PER SERVING:**
CALORIES: 307
FAT: 16G
CARBOHYDRATES: 14G
PROTEIN: 24G

PREPARATION TIME: 10 MINS
COOK TIME: 30 MINS

## INGREDIENTS:

- ○ 500g ground beef
- ○ 125g breadcrumbs
- ○ 60ml milk
- ○ 1 egg
- ○ 125g diced onion
- ○ 1 cloves of minced garlic
- ○ 1 tablespoon salt
- ○ 1 tablespoon black pepper
- ○ 60ml ketchup
- ○ 1 tablespoon brown sugar
- ○ 1 tablespoon mustard powder

## INSTRUCTIONS:

1. Preheat your air fryer to 180°C, for 5 minutes.
2. In a large bowl, mix together the ground beef, breadcrumbs, milk, egg, diced onion, minced garlic, salt, and black pepper.
3. Form the mixture into a loaf shape and place it in the air fryer.
4. In a small bowl, mix together the ketchup, brown sugar, and mustard powder. Spread the mixture over the meatloaf.
5. Cook the meatloaf for 25 minutes.
6. Remove from the air fryer and let it rest for 5 minutes before slicing and serving.
7. Serve with a side of your choice and enjoy the comfort food goodness!

# Breaded Pork Chops

Get ready to elevate your dinner game with this delicious Breaded Pork Chops recipe for the air fryer! This recipe is a fun and easy way to enjoy a classic dish without the hassle of stovetop cooking. The pork chops are coated in a crispy breading and then air-fried to perfection, resulting in a crispy exterior and a juicy and tender inside. This recipe is perfect for a week-night dinner or a special occasion and can be paired with a variety of sides such as roasted vegetables, mashed potatoes, or a salad. So, let's gather our ingredients and fire up our air fryers to make these delicious Breaded Pork Chops!

**NUTRITION PER SERVING:**
CALORIES: 522
FAT: 23G
CARBOHYDRATES: 36
PROTEIN: 35G

PREPARATION TIME: 10 MINS
COOK TIME: 25 MINS

## INGREDIENTS:

- O 4 pork chops (about 600g)
- O 80g all-purpose flour
- O 1 tablespoon salt
- O 1/2 tablespoon black pepper
- O 2 eggs
- O 60g breadcrumbs

## INSTRUCTIONS:

1. Preheat your air fryer to 180°C, for 5 minutes.
2. In a shallow dish, mix together the all-purpose flour, salt, and black pepper.
3. In another shallow dish, beat the eggs.
4. In a third shallow dish, place the breadcrumbs.
5. Dredge the pork chops in the all-purpose flour mixture, then the beaten eggs, and finally the breadcrumbs, making sure to coat evenly.
6. Place the breaded pork chops in the air fryer basket and cook for 15-20 minutes or until cooked through.
7. Remove from the air fryer and let rest for 5 minutes before serving.
8. Serve with a side of your choice and enjoy the crispy and juicy goodness!

# Coconut-Panko Crispy Chicken Strips

**SERVES 4**

Embark on a journey of taste-bud tingling deliciousness with this Coconut-Panko Crispy Chicken Strips recipe for the air fryer! This recipe is a fun and tropical twist on the classic chicken strips. The chicken is coated in a crispy coconut and panko breadcrumb crust and then air-fried to perfection, resulting in a crispy exterior and a juicy and tender inside. Served with a side of sweet chilli sauce, these chicken strips are sure to transport your taste buds to a tropical paradise. Perfect for a fun weeknight dinner or a party appetizer, these coconut-panko chicken strips will have everyone talking, and maybe even doing the hula dance.

So, let's gather our ingredients, fire up our air fryers, and get ready for a flavour explosion with these Coconut-Panko Crispy Chicken Strips!

**NUTRITION PER SERVING:**
CALORIES: 656
FAT: 11G
CARBOHYDRATES: 26G
PROTEIN: 35G

PREPARATION TIME: 10 MINS
COOK TIME: 20 MINS

## INGREDIENTS:

- 500g boneless, skinless chicken breasts, cut into strips
- 50g all-purpose flour
- 1 tablespoon salt
- 1/2 tablespoon black pepper
- 2 eggs
- 50g shredded coconut
- 100g panko breadcrumbs

## INSTRUCTIONS:

1. Preheat your air fryer to 180°C, for 5 minutes.
2. In a shallow dish, mix together the all-purpose flour, salt, and black pepper.
3. In another shallow dish, beat the eggs.
4. In a third shallow dish, mix together the shredded coconut and panko breadcrumbs.
5. Dredge the chicken strips in the all-purpose flour mixture, then the beaten eggs, and finally the coconut-panko mixture, making sure to coat evenly.
6. Place the crusted chicken strips in the air fryer basket and cook for 15-20 minutes.
7. Remove from the air fryer and let rest for 5 minutes before serving.
8. Serve with a side of your choice and enjoy the sweet and crispy goodness!

# Mustard-Crusted Pork Tenderloin

## SERVES 4

Looking for an easy and delicious way to cook pork tenderloin that is also healthy? Look no further because this recipe for air fryer mustard-crusted pork tenderloin is sure to be a hit! The mustard and breadcrumb crust gives the pork a delicious and crispy exterior, while the air fryer ensures that the pork is cooked to perfection.

**NUTRITION PER SERVING:**
CALORIES: 448
FAT: 16G
CARBOHYDRATES: 37G
PROTEIN: 35G

PREPARATION TIME: 10 MINS
COOK TIME: 25 MINS

## INGREDIENTS:

- 1 pork tenderloin (about 600g)
- 1 tablespoon olive oil
- 1 tablespoon salt
- 1/2 tablespoon black pepper
- 100ml Dijon mustard
- 60g breadcrumbs
- 2 cloves of minced garlic

## INSTRUCTIONS:

1. Preheat your air fryer to 180°C, for 5 minutes.
2. Season the pork tenderloin with 1 tablespoon of olive oil, salt, and black pepper.
3. In a small bowl, mix together the Dijon mustard and breadcrumbs. Spread the mixture over the pork tenderloin, making sure to coat evenly.
4. Place the pork tenderloin in the air fryer basket and cook for 20-25 minutes or until cooked through.
5. Remove the pork from the air fryer and let rest for 5 minutes before slicing.
6. Serve the pork tenderloin and enjoy the delicious and healthy meal!

# Rib Eye Steak

## SERVES 4

Craving a juicy and sizzling steak? Look no further because this recipe for air fryer rib eye steak is sure to exceed your wildest expectations! The rib eye steak is a flavourful and tender cut of beef that is perfect for grilling, and the air fryer is the perfect tool to cook it to perfection.

**NUTRITION PER SERVING:**
CALORIES: 738
FAT: 61G
CARBOHYDRATES: 0G
PROTEIN: 45G

PREPARATION TIME: 5 MINS
COOK TIME: 15 MINS

## INGREDIENTS:

- 2 rib eye steaks (about 500g)
- 1 tablespoon olive oil
- 1 tablespoon salt
- 1/2 tablespoon black pepper
- 1 tablespoon garlic powder
- 1 tablespoon onion powder

## INSTRUCTIONS:

1. Preheat your air fryer to 180°C, for 5 minutes.
2. Season the rib eye steaks with olive oil, salt, black pepper, garlic powder, and onion powder.
3. Place the steaks in the air fryer basket and cook for 12-15 minutes for medium-rare or until cooked through.
4. Remove the steaks from the air fryer and let them rest for 5 minutes before slicing.
5. Serve the steaks with a side of your choice and enjoy the juicy and flavourful goodness!

# Sesame-Crusted Cod with Snap Peas

## SERVES 4

This recipe for air fryer sesame-crusted cod with snap peas is sure to satisfy your cravings. The sesame crust gives the cod a crispy and flavourful exterior, while the snap peas add a burst of freshness to the dish. Grab your apron, let's go!

**NUTRITION PER SERVING:**
CALORIES: 389
FAT: 21G
CARBOHYDRATES: 17G
PROTEIN: 37G

PREPARATION TIME: 5 MINS
COOK TIME: 10 MINS

## INGREDIENTS:

- 4 cod fillets (about 600g)
- 60g all-purpose flour
- 1 tablespoon salt
- 1/2 tablespoon black pepper
- 2 eggs
- 65g sesame seeds
- 250g snap peas
- 1 tablespoon olive oil
- 1/4 tablespoon salt

## INSTRUCTIONS:

1. Preheat your air fryer to 180°C, for 5 minutes.
2. In a shallow dish, mix together the all-purpose flour, 1 tablespoon of salt, and black pepper.
3. In another shallow dish, beat the eggs.
4. In a third shallow dish, place the sesame seeds.
5. Dredge the cod fillets in the all-purpose flour mixture, then the beaten eggs, and finally the sesame seeds, making sure to coat evenly.
6. Place the cod fillets in the air fryer basket and cook for 8-10 minutes or until cooked through.
7. Remove the cod fillets from the air fryer and let them rest for 5 minutes before serving.
8. In a small pan, sauté the snap peas with 1 tablespoon of olive oil and 1/4 tablespoon of salt for 2-3 minutes or until they are tender.
9. Serve the cod fillets with the snap peas and enjoy the delicious and healthy meal!

# Chicken Tikka Masala with Boiled Rice

## SERVES 4

This recipe for Chicken Tikka Masala with Boiled Rice in an air fryer is a delectable and easy way to enjoy the classic Indian dish. Made with marinated chicken, a flavourful tomato-based sauce, and fluffy boiled rice, this recipe is perfect for a week night dinner or a special occasion. Plus, it's cooked all in one place, your trusty air fryer, so you can spend less time in the kitchen and more time with your loved ones.

**NUTRITION PER SERVING:**
CALORIES: 702
FAT: 23G
CARBOHYDRATES: 47G
PROTEIN: 31G

PREPARATION TIME: 10 MINS
COOK TIME: 30 MINS

## INGREDIENTS:

- 500g boneless, skinless chicken thighs, cut into bite-sized pieces
- 2 tablespoons plain yogurt
- 1 tablespoon lemon juice
- 1 tablespoon ginger paste
- 1 tablespoon garlic paste
- 1 tablespoon ground cumin
- 1 tablespoon ground coriander
- 1 tablespoon garam masala
- 1 tablespoon ground turmeric
- Salt and pepper, to taste
- 1 onion, finely chopped
- 2 cloves of garlic, minced
- 1 tablespoon tomato paste
- 240ml of canned diced tomatoes
- 240ml of heavy cream
- 100g basmati rice
- 200ml water
- Cooking spray

## INSTRUCTIONS:

1. Preheat your air fryer to 180°C, for 5 minutes.
2. In a mixing bowl, combine the yogurt, lemon juice, ginger paste, garlic paste, cumin, coriander, garam masala, turmeric, salt, and pepper. Mix well.
3. Add chicken to the bowl and coat well with the marinade. Let it sit for at least 30 minutes.
4. In the air fryer basket, mix together the onion, garlic, tomato paste, diced tomatoes, and heavy cream.
5. Add the chicken to the sauce, making sure it's coated well.
6. Add the washed rice and water in a separate container and place it on top of the chicken.
7. Cook for 25-30 minutes or until the chicken is cooked through and the rice is tender.
8. Serve and enjoy!

# Lemon Butter Chicken Thighs with Rice

## SERVES 4

Craving some Lemon Butter Chicken Thighs with Rice? This recipe is a luscious and easy dinner option that will impress your taste buds! Made with juicy chicken thighs, tangy lemon butter, and fluffy rice, this recipe is perfect for a week night dinner or a special occasion. Plus, it's cooked all in one place, your trusty air fryer, so you can spend less time in the kitchen and more time with your loved ones.

---

**NUTRITION PER SERVING:**
CALORIES: 675
FAT: 21G
CARBOHYDRATES: 46G
PROTEIN: 34G

---

PREPARATION TIME: 15 MINS
COOK TIME: 30 MINS

## INGREDIENTS:

- O 4 chicken thighs (about 500g)
- O 2 tablespoons butter, melted
- O 2 tablespoons lemon juice
- O 1 tablespoon garlic powder
- O 1 tablespoon dried thyme
- O Salt and pepper, to taste
- O 200g long-grain rice
- O 400ml chicken broth
- O Cooking spray

## INSTRUCTIONS:

1. Preheat your air fryer to 180°C, for 5 minutes.
2. In a mixing bowl, combine the melted butter, lemon juice, garlic powder, thyme, salt and pepper.
3. Dip the chicken thighs in the butter mixture, ensuring that both sides are coated.
4. In a separate mixing bowl, combine the rice and chicken broth.
5. Lightly coat the air fryer basket with cooking spray and place the chicken thighs in the basket.
6. Place the rice mixture on top of the chicken.
7. Cook in the air fryer for 25-30 minutes or until the chicken is cooked through and the rice is tender.
8. Serve and enjoy!

# Garlic & Herb Salmon with Broccoli

## SERVES 4

Filled with nutrition and packed with energy, this meal is very light and can be enjoyed for lunch and dinner. The mixed herbs add a fragrant and flavourful touch, while the broccoli provides a healthy and colourful side dish. It's an easy and satisfying meal that can be on the table in under 15 minutes.

**NUTRITION PER SERVING:**
CALORIES 264
FAT: 17G
CARBOHYDRATES: 0G
PROTEIN: 27G

PREPARATION TIME: 5 MINS
COOK TIME: 10 MINS

## INGREDIENTS

- 1 tablespoon of salt
- 1 tablespoon of pepper
- 1 tablespoon of mixed herbs
- 1 tablespoon of garlic granules
- 4 salmon fillets (we used 4 x 130g fillets), with the skin removed
- 1/2 tablespoon of olive oil
- 8 long stem broccoli

## INSTRUCTIONS

1. Preheat your air fryer to 180°C, for 5 minutes.
2. Mix the salt, pepper, mixed herbs and garlic granules in a bowl, then scatter onto a plate
3. Coat each salmon fillet with a little olive oil and roll in the seasoning
4. Place the fillets in the air fryer and cook for 10 mins, until cooked through.
5. Place the broccoli in the air fryer and cook for 5 mins
6. Plate the broccoli and fillets, and add extra seasoning before serving with quinoa or rice.

# Italian Penne Pasta

SERVES 4

This recipe is a delicious and easy way to make pasta in an air fryer. It's a classic Italian-style dish, with a flavourful marinara sauce, gooey melted cheese and a touch of Italian seasoning. You can use your favourite marinara sauce, and adjust the amount of seasoning or cheese to taste. You can also add some meat or vegetables like mushrooms, bell peppers or zucchini to make it more hearty.

**NUTRITION PER SERVING:**
CALORIES: 350
FAT: 12G
CARBOHYDRATES: 42G
PROTEIN: 18G

PREPARATION TIME: 5 MINS
COOK TIME: 10 MINS

## INGREDIENTS:

- 230g of Penne pasta
- 200ml of your favourite marinara sauce
- 50g of grated parmesan cheese
- 50g of grated mozzarella cheese
- 1 tablespoon of Italian seasoning
- 1/4 tablespoon of red pepper flakes (optional)
- Salt and pepper, to taste
- 1 tablespoon of olive oil
- 2 cloves of garlic, minced

## INSTRUCTIONS:

1. Cook the pasta according to package instructions until al dente. Drain and set aside.
2. In a small bowl, mix together the marinara sauce, parmesan cheese, mozzarella cheese, Italian seasoning, red pepper flakes, salt, pepper, olive oil and garlic.
3. Add the cooked pasta to the bowl with the sauce and toss to coat evenly.
4. Preheat the air fryer to 200°C, for 5 minutes.
5. Place the pasta in the air fryer basket and cook for 8-10 minutes or until the cheese is melted and the pasta is heated through.
6. Serve and enjoy!

# Thai Green Curry

## SERVES 4

It's Thai Green Curry Night! What makes this dish always a hit? The green curry paste gives such a rich and flavourful base, while the coconut milk adds a creamy and decadent touch. The vegetables add a colourful and healthy side dish. You can adjust the level of spiciness to your liking by adding or reducing the amount of curry paste.

**NUTRITION PER SERVING:**
CALORIES: 400
FAT: 30G
CARBOHYDRATES: 13G
PROTEIN: 25G

PREPARATION TIME: 5 MINS
COOK TIME: 15 MINS

## INGREDIENTS:

- 500g of boneless, skinless chicken breast, cut into bite-sized pieces
- 50g of sliced bell peppers (red, yellow or green)
- 50g of sliced onions
- 50g sliced mushrooms
- 50g of sliced zucchini
- 1 can of coconut milk
- 2 tablespoons of green curry paste
- 1 tablespoon of fish sauce
- 1 tablespoon of brown sugar
- 1 tablespoon of lime juice
- 2 cloves of garlic, minced
- Salt and pepper, to taste

## INSTRUCTIONS:

1. Preheat the air fryer to 200°C, for 5 minutes.
2. In a small bowl, mix together the coconut milk, green curry paste, fish sauce, brown sugar, lime juice, garlic, salt, and pepper.
3. Add the chicken, bell peppers, onions, mushrooms and zucchini to a large bowl and pour the curry sauce over the top. Toss to coat evenly.
4. Place the chicken and vegetables in the air fryer basket and cook for 12-15 minutes or until the chicken is cooked through and the vegetables are tender.
5. Serve over rice or noodles and garnish with fresh cilantro or basil if desired.

# Recipes – Dessert

# Profiteroles

Introducing the ultimate French delicacy made easy in your very own air fryer - air fryer profiteroles! These light and fluffy choux pastry balls filled with creamy custard and topped with rich chocolate will transport your taste buds straight to the streets of Paris. And the best part? They're made with simple, wholesome ingredients and are a healthier alternative to traditional deep-fried profiteroles.

**NUTRITION PER SERVING:**
CALORIES: 280
FAT: 20G
CARBOHYDRATES: 21G
PROTEIN: 4G

PREPARATION TIME: 15 MINS
COOK TIME: 20 MINS

## INGREDIENTS:

- ○ 150g all-purpose flour
- ○ 150ml water
- ○ 150ml whole milk
- ○ 150g unsalted butter
- ○ 4 large eggs
- ○ 1 teaspoon vanilla extract
- ○ 250ml whipped cream
- ○ Powdered sugar, for dusting

## INSTRUCTIONS:

1. Preheat the air fryer to 180°C, for 5 minutes.
2. In a medium saucepan, bring the water, milk, and butter to a boil. Once the butter is melted, add the flour and stir vigorously until a dough forms and pulls away from the sides of the pan.
3. Remove the pan from heat and let the dough cool for a few minutes.
4. Add the eggs, one at a time, stirring well after each addition. The dough should be smooth and glossy. Stir in the vanilla extract.
5. Using a pastry bag fitted with a round tip, pipe the dough into small rounds about the size of a golf ball. You can also use a spoon.
6. Place the profiteroles in the air fryer basket and cook for 15-20 minutes, or until golden brown and puffed up.
7. Let the profiteroles cool for a few minutes before filling them with whipped cream.
8. Dust with powdered sugar and serve your delicious air fryer profiteroles!

# Triple Chocolate Oatmeal Cookies

## SERVES 4

Get ready to indulge in a decadent and delicious treat with these air fryer triple-chocolate oatmeal cookies! They're the perfect combination of chewy oatmeal, rich chocolate, and a hint of crunch. Plus, they're made in the air fryer, so they're a healthier alternative to traditional baked cookies.

**NUTRITION PER SERVING:**
CALORIES: 312
FAT: 18G
CARBOHYDRATES: 36G
PROTEIN: 3G

PREPARATION TIME: 15 MINS
COOK TIME: 10 MINS

## INGREDIENTS:

- 100g rolled oats
- 60g all-purpose flour
- 45g cocoa powder
- 1g baking powder
- 1g baking soda
- 1g salt
- 120g unsalted butter, at room temperature
- 100g granulated sugar
- 100g brown sugar
- 1 large egg
- 1 teaspoon vanilla extract
- 90g dark chocolate chips
- 90g milk chocolate chips
- 90g white chocolate chips

## INSTRUCTIONS:

1. Preheat the air fryer to 180°C, for 5 minutes.
2. In a medium mixing bowl, combine the oats, all-purpose flour, cocoa powder, baking powder, baking soda, and salt. Mix until well combined.
3. In a separate mixing bowl, beat the butter, granulated sugar, and brown sugar until creamy.
4. Add the egg and vanilla extract to the butter mixture and mix until well combined.
5. Slowly add the dry ingredients to the butter mixture and mix until just combined.
6. Fold in the dark chocolate chips, milk chocolate chips, and white chocolate chips.
7. Using a cookie scoop or spoon, form the dough into balls and place them in the air fryer basket, making sure they are not touching each other.
8. Cook for 8-10 minutes or until golden brown.
9. Allow the cookies to cool for a few minutes before serving.

# Banana Cake

## SERVES 4

Turn your kitchen into a banana-licious paradise with this delicious Banana Cake recipe for the air fryer! This recipe is a fun and easy way to use up overripe bananas and turn them into a sweet and moist cake. The air fryer gives the cake a crispy crust while keeping the inside warm and fluffy.

Perfect for a weekend treat or a surprise dessert, this recipe is sure to delight your taste buds and your sense of humour. So, let's preheat our air fryers and get ready to bake up a storm with this Banana Cake recipe! And remember, if life gives you overripe bananas, make cake!

**NUTRITION PER SERVING:**
CALORIES: 240
FAT: 14G
CARBOHYDRATES: 29G
PROTEIN: 2G

PREPARATION TIME: 15 MINS
COOK TIME: 30 MINS

## INGREDIENTS:

- 200g gluten-free all-purpose flour
- 1 tablespoon baking powder
- 1 tablespoon baking soda
- 1 tablespoon ground cinnamon
- 1/4 tablespoon ground nutmeg
- 1/4 tablespoon salt
- 150g mashed ripe bananas (about 2 medium)
- 100g granulated sugar
- 100ml almond milk
- 60ml vegetable oil
- 1 tablespoon vanilla extract

## INSTRUCTIONS:

1. Preheat the air fryer to 180°C, for 5 minutes.
2. In a large mixing bowl, combine the all-purpose flour, baking powder, baking soda, cinnamon, nutmeg, and salt.
3. In a separate mixing bowl, combine the mashed bananas, sugar, almond milk, vegetable oil, and vanilla extract. Mix well.
4. Slowly add the wet ingredients to the dry ingredients, stirring until just combined.
5. Pour the batter into an oiled air fryer safe cake pan.
6. Set the air fryer to 180°C and bake the cake for 25-30 minutes, or until a toothpick inserted into the centre comes out clean.
7. Let the cake cool for at least 10 minutes before removing it from the pan and serving.

# Apple Cider Doughnut Bites

SERVES 4

Introducing the sizzlin' hot, fresh out of the air fryer, Apple Cider Doughnut Bites. These little nuggets of deliciousness will make your kitchen smell like a fall wonderland and have your friends and family begging for the recipe. So grab your air fryer and let's get fryin'!

**NUTRITION PER SERVING:**
CALORIES: 80
FAT: 3G
CARBOHYDRATES: 13G
PROTEIN: 2G

PREPARATION TIME: 15 MINS
COOK TIME: 10 MINS

## INGREDIENTS:

- 250g all-purpose flour
- 2 tablespoons baking powder
- 1 tablespoon ground cinnamon
- 1/4 tablespoon ground nutmeg
- 1/4 tablespoon salt
- 1/4 tablespoon ground ginger
- 200ml unsweetened apple cider
- 20g granulated sugar
- 1 egg
- 2 tablespoons unsalted butter, melted
- 1 tablespoon vanilla extract

## INSTRUCTIONS:

1. Preheat the air fryer to 190°C.
2. In a large mixing bowl, combine the all-purpose flour, baking powder, cinnamon, nutmeg, salt, and ginger.
3. In a separate mixing bowl, whisk together the apple cider, sugar, egg, melted butter, and vanilla extract.
4. Add the wet ingredients to the dry ingredients and stir until just combined.
5. Roll the dough out on a all-purpose floured surface to 1/2 inch thickness.
6. Use a round cookie cutter to cut out doughnut shapes.
7. Place the doughnut bites in the air fryer, making sure to not overcrowd them.
8. Cook for 6-8 minutes or until golden brown.
9. Once done, take the doughnuts out of the air fryer and let them cool for a few minutes before serving.

# Mini Blueberry Scones

Are you ready to treat yourself to some warm and flaky mini scones straight out of your air fryer? These mini blueberry scones are the perfect breakfast or brunch treat, and they're so easy to make!

**NUTRITION PER SERVING:**
CALORIES: 150
FAT: 9G
CARBOHYDRATES: 15G
PROTEIN: 2G

PREPARATION TIME: 20 MINS
COOK TIME: 10 MINS

## INGREDIENTS:

○ 200g all-purpose flour
○ 2 tablespoons baking powder
○ 1/4 tablespoon salt
○ 40g granulated sugar
○ 40g unsalted butter, chilled and diced
○ 100g fresh blueberries
○ 80g heavy cream
○ 1 tablespoon vanilla extract

## INSTRUCTIONS:

1. Preheat the air fryer to 180°C, for 5 minutes.
2. In a large mixing bowl, combine the all-purpose flour, baking powder, salt, and sugar.
3. Cut in the butter with a pastry cutter or use your hands to knead the mix until coarse and flaky.
4. Fold in the blueberries.
5. In a separate mixing bowl, whisk together the cream and vanilla extract.
6. Add the wet ingredients to the dry ingredients and stir until just combined.
7. Knead the dough on a all-purpose floured surface until it comes together.
8. Roll out the dough to about 1/2 inch thickness.
9. Use a round cookie cutter to cut out mini scones.
10. Place the scones in the air fryer, making sure to not overcrowd them.
11. Cook for 8-10 minutes or until golden brown.
12. Once done, take the scones out of the air fryer and let them cool for a few minutes before serving.
13. Serve these mini blueberry scones warm with some butter or jam for the ultimate breakfast treat. These scones are perfect to enjoy with your morning coffee or tea and will be sure to impress your family and friends.

# Home-made Cinnamon Churros

## SERVES 4

It's time to indulge in some deliciously irresistible, crispy and warm Cinnamon Churros straight out of your air fryer! These Churros are easy to make and will be sure to satisfy your sweet cravings. Serve these warm and sweet Cinnamon Churros with a cup of hot chocolate or coffee for the ultimate comfort dessert. Don't be shy, grab as many as you want, we won't judge!

**NUTRITION PER CHURRO:**
CALORIES: 250
FAT: 14G
CARBOHYDRATES: 27G
PROTEIN: 4G

PREPARATION TIME: 10 MINS
COOK TIME: 10 MINS

## INGREDIENTS:

- ○ 250g all-purpose flour
- ○ 1 tablespoon baking powder
- ○ 1/2 tablespoon salt
- ○ 250ml water
- ○ 60g unsalted butter
- ○ 3 large eggs
- ○ 1 tablespoon vanilla extract
- ○ 50g granulated sugar
- ○ 2 tablespoons ground cinnamon
- ○ Oil for frying

1.  Preheat the air fryer to 190°C.
2.  In a medium mixing bowl, combine all-purpose flour, baking powder, and salt.
3.  In a medium saucepan, bring water and butter to a boil. Remove from heat and add the all-purpose flour mixture, stirring until a dough forms.
4.  Add the eggs, one at a time, mixing well after each addition, until the dough is smooth and glossy. Stir in vanilla extract
5.  Place the dough into a pastry bag fitted with a large star tip.
6.  Pipe the dough into the air fryer, forming the churros into 4-5 inches long.
7.  Air-fry the churros for 8-10 minutes or until golden brown.
8.  While the churros are still warm, mix together sugar and cinnamon in a shallow dish. Roll the churros in the cinnamon sugar mixture.
9.  Once done, take the churros out of the air fryer and let them cool for a few minutes before serving.

# Peanut Butter & Jelly S'mores

## SERVES 4

These Peanut Butter & Jelly S'mores are the perfect treat for a cosy night in or for a fun family dessert night. You can also try different combinations of spreads and nuts for a unique twist on the classic s'more. So go ahead and treat yourself to this delicious and easy treat!

**NUTRITION PER SERVING:**
CALORIES: 360
FAT: 16G
CARBOHYDRATES: 26G
PROTEIN: 5G

PREPARATION TIME: 10 MINS
COOK TIME: 5 MINS

## INGREDIENTS:

○ 4 Graham crackers
○ 4 tablespoons peanut butter
○ 4 tablespoons jelly or jam
○ 4 marshmallows

## INSTRUCTIONS:

1. Preheat the air fryer to 180°C, for 5 minutes.
2. Place 2 graham crackers on a plate or cutting board.
3. Spread 1 tablespoon of peanut butter on one cracker and 1 tablespoon of jelly or jam on the other.
4. Place a marshmallow on top of one of the crackers and sandwich the two crackers together.
5. Place the s'more in the air fryer.
6. Cook for 2-3 minutes or until the marshmallow is golden brown and gooey.
7. Once done, take the s'more out of the air fryer and let it cool for a few minutes before serving.

# Home-made Apple Pies

## SERVES 4

Get ready to enjoy a warm, gooey, and delicious mini apple pie straight out of your air fryer! These pies are the perfect fall treat and are sure to impress your family and friends. Plus, they're a healthier alternative to traditional deep-fried pies, so you can indulge without any guilt. Enjoy your home-made air fryer apple pies! Serve them warm with a scoop of vanilla ice cream for an extra special treat.

**NUTRITION PER SERVING:**
CALORIES: 225
FAT: 12G
CARBOHYDRATES: 27G
PROTEIN: 2G

PREPARATION TIME: 15 MINS
COOK TIME: 15 MINS

## INGREDIENTS:

- ○ 2 large granny smith apples, peeled and diced (about 500 grams)
- ○ 30g granulated sugar
- ○ 1 teaspoon ground cinnamon
- ○ 1/4 teaspoon nutmeg
- ○ 1/4 teaspoon allspice
- ○ 30g all-purpose flour
- ○ 30g unsalted butter, cut into small pieces
- ○ 60ml apple juice
- ○ 1 package (400 grams) store-bought pie crust

## INSTRUCTIONS:

1. Preheat the air fryer to 180°C, for 5 minutes.
2. In a large mixing bowl, combine the diced apples, sugar, cinnamon, nutmeg, allspice, all-purpose flour, butter, and apple juice. Mix until the ingredients are well combined.
3. Roll out the pie crust on a all-purpose floured surface to a thickness of about 1/8 inch.
4. Using a round cookie cutter or glass, cut out circles of dough.
5. Place a spoonful of the apple mixture in the centre of each dough circle.
6. Fold the dough in half and press the edges together to seal the pies.
7. Place the pies in the air fryer basket, making sure they are not touching each other.
8. Cook for 12-15 minutes or until golden brown.
9. Allow the pies to cool for a few minutes before serving.

# Italian Tiramisu

## SERVES 8

This recipe is an easy and delicious to make traditional Italian tiramisu in an air fryer. The mascarpone cheese and heavy cream give it a creamy and rich texture, while the espresso and Marsala give it a unique and delicious flavour. The ladyfingers are softened by the espresso and Marsala mixture, giving it a moist texture. It's a perfect dessert to finish off a dinner party or a romantic dinner. Tiramisu is a rich and sweet dessert, it's best to consume it in moderation.

**NUTRITION PER SERVING (BASED ON 8 SERVINGS):**
CALORIES: 280
FAT: 21G
CARBOHYDRATES: 16G
PROTEIN: 5G

PREPARATION TIME: 10 MINS
COOK TIME: 10 MINS

## INGREDIENTS:

- 500g of mascarpone cheese
- 80g of heavy cream
- 100g of powdered sugar
- 1 tablespoon of vanilla extract
- 40g of espresso or strong coffee
- 100ml of Marsala or other sweet wine
- 1 package of ladyfingers
- Cocoa powder, for dusting

## INSTRUCTIONS:

1. In a large bowl, mix together the mascarpone cheese, heavy cream, powdered sugar and vanilla extract until smooth.
2. In a separate bowl, mix together the espresso and Marsala.
3. Dip the ladyfingers into the espresso mixture, being sure to coat both sides.
4. Layer the ladyfingers in the bottom of the air fryer basket, breaking them as needed to fit.
5. Spread a layer of the mascarpone mixture over the ladyfingers.
6. Repeat the process, layering ladyfingers and mascarpone mixture until all ingredients are used.
7. Dust the top with cocoa powder.
8. Preheat the air fryer to 175°C, for 5 minutes.
9. Place the tiramisu in the air fryer and cook for 8-10 minutes or until heated through and the cocoa powder is lightly toasted.
10. Allow to cool slightly before serving.

# Coconut Macaroons

These Coconut Macaroons are a perfect treat for anyone who loves coconut and wants a gluten-free and vegan option. Serve them on their own or with a cup of tea or coffee for a sweet and satisfying snack. And, remember, if you're feeling cheeky, go ahead and have a second one, or even a third!

**NUTRITION PER SERVING:**
CALORIES: 90
FAT: 7G
CARBOHYDRATES: 7G
PROTEIN: 1G

PREPARATION TIME: 10 MINS
COOK TIME: 10 MINS

## INGREDIENTS:

- 200g shredded coconut
- 125ml full-fat coconut milk
- 100g granulated sugar
- 1 tablespoon vanilla extract
- 1/4 tablespoon salt
- 30g cornstarch

## INSTRUCTIONS:

1. Preheat the air fryer to 180°C, for 5 minutes.
2. In a large mixing bowl, combine the shredded coconut, coconut milk, sugar, vanilla extract, and salt.
3. Mix in cornstarch to the mixture until it forms into a thick dough.
4. Using a cookie scoop or spoon, form the dough into 1-inch balls and place them in the air fryer.
5. Cook for 8-10 minutes or until golden brown.
6. Once done, take the macaroons out of the air fryer and let them cool for a few minutes before serving.

# Dessert Empanadas

Welcome to the world of air fryer empanadas, where flaky pastry meets gooey, sweet fruit filling, and everything is cooked to perfection in a fraction of the time it takes to bake them in the oven. These empanadas are not only delicious but also a great way to trick your friends into thinking you have mad baking skills, but shh, we won't tell if you don't! Let's get started and make some mouthwatering, air fryer dessert empanadas that will have everyone asking for seconds (or thirds).

**NUTRITION PER SERVING:**
CALORIES: 210
FAT: 8G
CARBOHYDRATES: 32G
PROTEIN: 2G

PREPARATION TIME: 35 MINS
COOK TIME: 15 MINS

## INGREDIENTS:

- 125g all-purpose flour
- 1g salt
- 60g unsalted butter, chilled and diced
- 60ml cold water
- 200g brown sugar
- 300g diced mixed fruit (such as apples, peaches, and berries)
- 1 tablespoon vanilla extract
- 1 tablespoon ground cinnamon
- Egg wash (1 beaten egg mixed with 1 tablespoon of water)
- Powdered sugar for dusting

## INSTRUCTIONS:

1. Preheat the air fryer to 180°C, for 5 minutes.
2. In a large bowl, mix together all-purpose flour and salt.
3. Add in diced butter and use your fingers to work it into the all-purpose flour mixture until it resembles coarse crumbs.
4. Slowly add in cold water, a tablespoon at a time, until the dough comes together.
5. Knead the dough briefly on a all-purpose floured surface until it is smooth.
6. Wrap the dough in plastic wrap and refrigerate for at least 30 minutes.
7. In a separate bowl, mix together brown sugar, diced fruit, vanilla extract, and ground cinnamon.
8. Roll out the dough on a all-purpose floured surface to about 3mm thickness.
9. Use a round cutter or a glass to cut out circles of dough.
10. Place a spoonful of the fruit mixture onto one half of each dough circle, leaving a small border around the edges.
11. Brush the edges with the egg wash and fold the other half of the dough over the filling, pressing the 11. edges to seal.
12. Place the empanadas in the air fryer basket and brush the tops with the remaining egg wash.
13. Air fry for 12-15 minutes or until the empanadas are golden brown.
14. Once done, dust the empanadas with powdered sugar before serving.

# Banana Bites

## SERVES 4

Who says healthy snacks have to be boring? These air fryer banana bites are the perfect combination of sweet and crispy. They are so easy to make, even a monkey could do it (get it?). You can enjoy them as a quick breakfast, a sweet treat or even a dessert. One thing is for sure, they will disappear faster than a banana in a bunch of monkeys!

**NUTRITION PER SERVING:**
CALORIES: 120
FAT: 5G
CARBOHYDRATES: 22G
PROTEIN: 1G

PREPARATION TIME: 5 MINS
COOK TIME: 10 MINS

## INGREDIENTS:

- 2 bananas
- 2 tablespoons melted butter
- 2 tablespoons brown sugar
- 1 tablespoon cinnamon
- Pinch of salt

## INSTRUCTIONS:

1. Preheat the air fryer to 180°C, for 5 minutes.
2. Peel and slice the bananas into bite-sized pieces.
3. In a small bowl, mix together melted butter, brown sugar, cinnamon, and salt.
4. Dip each banana piece into the butter mixture, making sure it's evenly coated.
5. Place the banana bites in the air fryer basket and cook for 8-10 minutes or until golden brown and crispy.
6. Serve warm and enjoy your delicious and healthy treat!

# Banana Fritters

## SERVES 8

This recipe is a delicious and easy way to make banana fritters in an air fryer. These fritters are crispy on the outside and soft and sweet inside. The addition of cinnamon gives it a unique and delicious flavour.

They are a perfect treat to enjoy as a snack or dessert. You can also dust them with powdered sugar or drizzle them with chocolate or caramel sauce to make them more decadent.

**NUTRITION PER SERVING (BASED ON 8 SERVINGS):**
CALORIES: 110
FAT: 3G
CARBOHYDRATES: 22G
PROTEIN: 2G

PREPARATION TIME: 5 MINS
COOK TIME: 10 MINS

## INGREDIENTS:

- O 2 ripe bananas, mashed
- O 50g all-purpose flour
- O 50g of cornstarch
- O 40g of sugar
- O 1/2 tablespoon of baking powder
- O 1/4 tablespoon of salt
- O 1/4 tablespoon of ground cinnamon
- O 1/4 tablespoon of vanilla extract
- O 1 large egg
- O Olive Oil

## INSTRUCTIONS:

1. Preheat the air fryer to 200°C, for 5 minutes.
2. In a medium bowl, mix together the mashed bananas, all-purpose flour, cornstarch, sugar, baking powder, salt, cinnamon, vanilla extract and egg.
3. Using a tablespoon, drop spoonfuls of the batter into the air fryer basket. Be sure to leave enough space between each fritter.
4. Brush the fritters with oil.
5. Cook for 6-8 minutes or until golden brown and cooked through.
6. Remove from the air fryer and let cool slightly before serving.

# Apricot and Apple Crisp

## SERVES 4

Craving something sweet and comforting? Look no further! This air fryer apricot and apple crisp is the perfect treat for any occasion. With its warm and gooey fruit filling and crispy and buttery topping, it will have your taste buds doing the cha-cha. Plus, it's healthier than the traditional version, cooked in an air fryer. But don't let that fool you, it's still as delicious as ever. Just be careful not to burn your tongue, it's hot and bubbly!

**NUTRITION PER SERVING:**
CALORIES: 270
FAT: 11G
CARBOHYDRATES: 44G
PROTEIN: 2G

PREPARATION TIME: 10 MINS
COOK TIME: 20 MINS

## INGREDIENTS:

- 300g apricots, pitted and sliced
- 300g apples, peeled and sliced
- 100g granulated sugar
- 1 tablespoon vanilla extract
- 1 tablespoon ground cinnamon
- Pinch of salt
- 60g all-purpose flour
- 60g rolled oats
- 60g unsalted butter, diced

## INSTRUCTIONS:

1. Preheat the air fryer to 180°C, for 5 minutes.
2. In a large mixing bowl, combine apricots, apples, sugar, vanilla extract, cinnamon, and salt.
3. Mix together all-purpose flour, oats, and butter in a separate bowl until it forms a crumbly mixture.
4. Place the apricot and apple mixture in the air fryer basket.
5. Sprinkle the all-purpose flour and oat mixture over the fruit.
6. Cook for 15-20 minutes or until the fruit is tender and the topping is golden brown.
7. Allow the crisp to cool slightly before serving.
8. Serve warm with a scoop of vanilla ice cream or whipped cream if desired.

# Recipes – Snacks

# Pasta Chips

Are you tired of boring chips? Look no further! These air fryer pasta chips are here to shake up your snack game. They're crispy, flavourful and perfect for dipping in your favourite sauce. Plus, you can enjoy them guilt-free as they are cooked in an air fryer. Just don't blame me if you can't stop munching on them, they are that addictive! This recipe is a great way to use up leftover pasta or to make a new twist on your pasta night, who needs boring pasta when you can have crispy pasta chips?

**NUTRITION PER SERVING:**
CALORIES: 260
FAT: 13G
CARBOHYDRATES: 30G
PROTEIN: 7G

PREPARATION TIME: 10 MINS
COOK TIME: 10 MINS

## INGREDIENTS:

- 200g uncooked pasta (such as fusilli, or any other small pasta shape)
- 2 tablespoons (30ml) olive oil
- 1 tablespoon (5g) dried oregano
- 1 tablespoon (5g) garlic powder
- Salt and pepper, to taste

## INSTRUCTIONS:

1. Preheat the air fryer to 180°C, for 5 minutes.
2. Cook the pasta according to package instructions until al dente.
3. Drain and rinse the pasta under cold water to stop the cooking process.
4. In a mixing bowl, toss the pasta with olive oil, oregano, garlic powder, salt, and pepper.
5. Place the pasta in the air fryer basket in a single layer.
6. Cook for 8-10 minutes or until the pasta is crispy and golden brown.
7. Remove the pasta from the air fryer and let it cool for a few minutes before serving.
8. Enjoy your crispy pasta chips as a snack, or with your favourite dip.

# Monkey Bread

## SERVES 4

Calling all monkey bread lovers! Your wildest dreams are about to come true with this recipe for Monkey Bread straight out of the air fryer. No more waiting for the oven to preheat or dealing with unevenly cooked gooey-ness. Just toss it in the fryer and before you can say "bananas", you'll have a warm, pull-apart treat that will have your taste buds swinging from the rafters. Get ready to monkey around with this deliciously easy recipe!

**NUTRITION PER SERVING:**
CALORIES: 260
FAT: 13G
CARBOHYDRATES: 36G
PROTEIN: 2G

PREPARATION TIME: 15 MINS
COOK TIME: 15 MINS

## INGREDIENTS:

- 1 can of refrigerated biscuits (450g)
- 100g granulated sugar
- 1 tablespoon cinnamon
- 110g unsalted butter
- 100g light brown sugar

## INSTRUCTIONS:

1. Preheat the air fryer to 180°C, for 5 minutes.
2. Cut the biscuits into quarters and set aside.
3. In a small bowl, mix together the granulated sugar and cinnamon.
4. In a separate bowl, melt the butter and stir in the brown sugar.
5. Dip the biscuit quarters in the butter mixture, then roll them in the cinnamon sugar mixture.
6. Place the coated biscuit pieces in the air fryer basket, making sure they're not touching.
7. Cook for 10-12 minutes, or until the biscuits are golden brown and the glaze is bubbly.
8. Serve immediately and enjoy!

# Shortbread

## SERVES 4

These buttery, crumbly, and oh-so-delicious cookies are sure to satisfy your sweet tooth and make you the star of your next snack time. Plus, you can enjoy them without feeling guilty, as they are cooked in an air fryer! Just don't blame me if you eat the entire batch in one sitting, they are that addictive!

**NUTRITION PER SERVING:**
CALORIES: 230
FAT: 8G
CARBOHYDRATES: 14G
PROTEIN: 1G

PREPARATION TIME: 10 MINS
COOK TIME: 15 MINS

## INGREDIENTS:

- ○ 225g unsalted butter, at room temperature
- ○ 100g granulated sugar
- ○ 2 tablespoons (10ml) vanilla extract
- ○ 250g all-purpose flour
- ○ Pinch of salt

## INSTRUCTIONS:

1. Preheat the air fryer to 150°C.
2. In a large mixing bowl, beat butter and sugar together until creamy.
3. Add in vanilla extract and mix well.
4. In a separate bowl, mix together all-purpose flour and salt. Gradually add the all-purpose flour mixture to the butter mixture, mixing until it forms a dough.
5. Roll out the dough on a lightly all-purpose floured surface to about 1cm thickness.
6. Use a cookie cutter or glass to cut out the cookies.
7. Place the cookies in the air fryer basket and cook for 10-12 minutes or until the edges are golden brown.
8. Allow the cookies to cool slightly before removing them from the air fryer.
9. Enjoy your delicious and crispy shortbread cookies!

# Oatmeal and Raisin Cookies

## SERVES 4

Air fryer oatmeal and raisin cookies are a delicious and healthy alternative to traditional baked cookies. Made with wholesome ingredients such as rolled oats, whole wheat flour, and raisins, these cookies are a great option for a snack or breakfast on the go. Plus, using an air fryer to cook them means they'll have less fat and be a bit healthier than traditional baked cookies. You can also add different types of nuts or seeds to the dough to make it even more nutritious. It's a great recipe for a healthy and delicious snack or breakfast on the go, a perfect way to start the day with healthy ingredients.

Here is a recipe for air fryer oatmeal and raisin cookies that yields about 12 cookies.

**NUTRITION PER SERVING:**
CALORIES: 120
FAT: 7G
CARBOHYDRATES: 14G
PROTEIN: 2G

PREPARATION TIME: 10 MINS
COOK TIME: 15 MINS

## INGREDIENTS:

- O  100g rolled oats
- O  100g whole wheat flour
- O  50g brown sugar
- O  1 tablespoon baking powder
- O  1/4 tablespoon salt
- O  1 tablespoon cinnamon
- O  80ml vegetable oil
- O  1 egg
- O  1 tablespoon vanilla extract
- O  100g raisins

## INSTRUCTIONS:

1. Preheat the air fryer to 150°C.
2. In a large mixing bowl, beat butter and sugar together until creamy.
3. Add in vanilla extract and mix well.
4. In a separate bowl, mix together all-purpose flour and salt. Gradually add the all-purpose flour mixture to the butter mixture, mixing until it forms a dough.
5. Roll out the dough on a lightly all-purpose floured surface to about 1cm thickness.
6. Use a cookie cutter or cooking template to cut out the cookies.
7. Place the cookies in the air fryer basket and cook for 10-12 minutes or until the edges are golden brown.
8. Allow the cookies to cool slightly before removing them from the air fryer.
9. Enjoy your delicious and crispy shortbread cookies!

# Recipes – Sides & Appetizers

# Bagel Bites

**SERVES 4**

Upgrade your snack game with these delicious and stylish air fryer bagel bites. These mini bagels are loaded with gooey cheese, savoury pizza sauce and seasoned with oregano, salt and pepper. Cooked to perfection in an air fryer, they are crispy on the outside and soft on the inside. Perfect for a quick lunch, a party appetizer or a snack, these bagel bites will be a hit among your friends and family. So why not elevate your snacking experience with these air fryer bagel bites?

**NUTRITION PER SERVING:**
CALORIES: 280
FAT: 11G
CARBOHYDRATES: 33G
PROTEIN: 12G

PREPARATION TIME: 5 MINS
COOK TIME: 10 MINS

## INGREDIENTS:

- ○ 4 mini bagels, halved (200g)
- ○ 125g pizza sauce
- ○ 100g shredded mozzarella cheese
- ○ 30g grated Parmesan cheese
- ○ 15g diced pepperoni (optional)
- ○ 5g dried oregano
- ○ Salt and pepper, to taste

## INSTRUCTIONS:

1. Preheat the air fryer to 180°C, for 5 minutes.
2. Spread the pizza sauce on each bagel half.
3. Sprinkle mozzarella, Parmesan cheese, pepperoni (if using), oregano, salt and pepper on top of the sauce.
4. Place the bagel bites in the air fryer basket and cook for 8-10 minutes or until the cheese is 5. melted and the bagel is toasted.
5. Remove the bagel bites from the air fryer and let them cool for a few minutes before serving.
6. Enjoy your delicious and crispy bagel bites!

# Cream Cheese Stuffed Peppers

**SERVES 4**

These air fryer cream cheese stuffed peppers are the perfect way to satisfy your cravings for something creamy, cheesy and flavourful. Plus, you can enjoy them without feeling guilty, as they are cooked in an air fryer. Just don't blame me if you eat the entire batch in one sitting, they are that addictive! Perfect for a side dish or a meal by itself, this recipe will make you love your veggies in a whole new way.

**NUTRITION PER SERVING:**
CALORIES: 230
FAT: 20G
CARBOHYDRATES: 8G
PROTEIN: 8G

PREPARATION TIME: 10 MINS
COOK TIME: 15 MINS

## INGREDIENTS:

- ○ 4 bell peppers, halved and seeded
- ○ 200g cream cheese, at room temperature
- ○ 60ml milk
- ○ 30g grated Parmesan cheese
- ○ 2 cloves of garlic, minced
- ○ 1/4 tablespoon (1g) red pepper flakes (optional)
- ○ Salt and pepper, to taste

## INSTRUCTIONS:

1. Preheat the air fryer to 180°C, for 5 minutes.
2. In a mixing bowl, mix together cream cheese, milk, Parmesan cheese, garlic, red pepper flakes (if using), salt, and pepper.
3. Stuff each pepper half with the cream cheese mixture.
4. Place the stuffed peppers in the air fryer basket and cook for 12-15 minutes or until the peppers are tender and the filling is hot and bubbly.
5. Remove the peppers from the air fryer and let them cool for a few minutes before serving.
6. Enjoy your delicious and creamy stuffed peppers!

# Crispy Breaded Mushrooms

## SERVES 4

Here's a delicious and easy way to make crispy breaded mushrooms in an air fryer. The mushrooms are coated in a mixture of all-purpose flour, breadcrumbs, and grated Parmesan cheese, which gives them a crispy and savoury texture. Air frying them at a high temperature allows them to cook quickly and evenly, without the need for deep-frying. They're a perfect side dish to go with any meal, or a great appetizer for parties.

**NUTRITION PER SERVING:**
CALORIES: 60
FAT: 2G
CARBOHYDRATES: 8G
PROTEIN: 3G

PREPARATION TIME: 5 MINS
COOK TIME: 15 MINS

## INGREDIENTS:

- ◯ 200g mushrooms (sliced)
- ◯ 30g all-purpose flour
- ◯ 30g breadcrumbs
- ◯ 15g grated Parmesan cheese
- ◯ 2ml olive oil
- ◯ 2ml water
- ◯ Salt and pepper (to taste)

## INSTRUCTIONS:

1. Preheat the air fryer to 180°C, for 5 minutes.
2. In a bowl, mix together all-purpose flour, breadcrumbs, Parmesan cheese, salt, and pepper.
3. In a separate bowl, mix together olive oil and water.
4. Dip the mushroom slices in the liquid mixture, then coat them in the breadcrumb mixture.
5. Place the mushrooms in the air fryer basket, making sure they are not overlapping.
6. Air fry for 10-15 minutes, or until golden brown and crispy.
7. Serve hot and enjoy!

# Jalapeno Poppers

**SERVES 4**

These jalapenos peppers are stuffed with a mixture of cream cheese and cheddar cheese, which adds a creamy and spicy flavour. They are then coated in a mixture of all-purpose flour and breadcrumbs, which gives them a crispy texture. Air frying them at a high temperature allows them to cook quickly and evenly, without the need for deep-frying. They are perfect as a snack or an appetizer for parties. Be careful when handling jalapenos, as they can be quite spicy. You can adjust the heat level to your taste by removing more or less of the seeds and membranes before stuffing.

**NUTRITION PER SERVING:**
CALORIES: 120
FAT: 10G
CARBOHYDRATES: 5G
PROTEIN: 4G

PREPARATION TIME: 10 MINS
COOK TIME: 10 MINS

## INGREDIENTS:

- 12 jalapeno peppers (halved and seeded)
- 60g cream cheese (softened)
- 30g shredded cheddar cheese
- 15g all-purpose flour
- 15g breadcrumbs
- 1ml olive oil
- Salt and pepper (to taste)

## INSTRUCTIONS:

1. Preheat the air fryer to 180°C, for 5 minutes.
2. In a bowl, mix together cream cheese, cheddar cheese, salt, and pepper.
3. Stuff each jalapeno half with the cheese mixture.
4. In a separate bowl, mix together all-purpose flour, breadcrumbs, salt, and pepper.
5. Dip the stuffed jalapenos in the all-purpose flour mixture, then coat them in breadcrumbs.
6. Place the jalapeno poppers in the air fryer basket, making sure they are not overlapping.
7. Brush the tops with olive oil.
8. Air fry for 8-10 minutes, or until golden brown and crispy.
9. Serve hot and enjoy!

# Stuffed Mushrooms

**SERVES 4**

Get ready to elevate your appetizer game with this delicious and easy recipe for air fryer Stuffed Mushrooms! These mushrooms are the perfect combination of savoury and cheesy, making them the perfect addition to any meal or party spread. Plus, by using an air fryer, you can enjoy all the flavour without all the guilt of deep-frying.

**NUTRITION PER SERVING:**
CALORIES: 90
FAT: 8G
CARBOHYDRATES: 3G
PROTEIN: 3G

PREPARATION TIME: 10 MINS
COOK TIME: 10 MINS

## INGREDIENTS:

- 8 medium-sized mushrooms
- 60ml olive oil
- 25g grated Parmesan cheese
- 25g breadcrumbs
- 30g chopped spinach
- 30g crumbled feta cheese
- 2 cloves of garlic, minced
- Salt and pepper to taste

## INSTRUCTIONS:

1. Preheat the air fryer to 180°C, for 5 minutes.
2. Remove the mushroom stems and set the caps aside. Finely chop the mushroom stems.
3. In a pan, heat the olive oil over medium heat. Add the mushroom stems, garlic, spinach, salt, and pepper. Cook until the mushrooms are tender, about 5 minutes.
4. In a mixing bowl, combine the cooked mushroom mixture, breadcrumbs, Parmesan cheese, and feta cheese. Mix well.
5. Stuff each mushroom cap with the mixture.
6. Place the mushrooms in the air fryer basket and cook for about 10 minutes or until the mushrooms are tender and the filling is golden brown.
7. Serve hot and enjoy!

# Weekly Meal Plan

This plan is designed to help you cook healthier meals with the use of an air fryer. Cooking with an air fryer is a great way to reduce the amount of oil needed for frying, resulting in healthier and lower-calorie meals. Our plan includes a variety of delicious recipes that are easy to prepare and perfect for busy week-nights. With this plan, you'll be able to enjoy your favourite foods while also taking care of your health. Let's get started!

**Monday**
Breakfast: Strawberry Oatmeal
Dinner: Beef Stroganoff with Boiled Rice
Dessert: Home-made Apple Pies
**Calorie count: 1255**

**Tuesday**
Breakfast: Breakfast Puffed Egg Tarts
Dinner: Lemon Butter Chicken Thighs with Rice
Dessert: Coconut Macaroons
**Calorie count: 956**

**Wednesday**
Breakfast: Blueberry Porridge
Dinner: Katsu Chicken
Dessert: Italian Tiramisu
**Calorie count: 1424**

**Thursday**
Breakfast: Full English Breakfast
Dinner: Crispy Duck and Pancakes with Hoisin Sauce
Dessert: Triple Chocolate Oatmeal Cookies
**Calorie count: 1752**

**Friday**
Breakfast: Cheese & Onion Omelette
Dinner: Coconut-Panko Crispy Chicken Strips
Dessert: Peanut Butter & Jelly S'mores
**Calorie count: 1166**

Most women are recommended to intake 1,600–2,400 daily calories in order to maintain their weight. Most men are recommended to intake 2,000–3,000 calories per day.

Subject to body mass, height and age.

Choose from any snack, sides and appetisers in this cookbook to fill the gaps and maintain a balanced and healthy diet.

# Disclaimer

This book contains opinions and ideas of the author and is meant to teach the reader informative and helpful knowledge while due care should be taken by the user in the application of the information provided. The instructions and strategies are possibly not right for every reader and there is no guarantee that they work for everyone. Using this book and implementing the information/ recipes therein contained is explicitly your own responsibility and risk. This work with all its contents, does not guarantee correctness, completion, quality or correctness of the provided information. Misinformation or misprints cannot be completely eliminated.

# EXCLUSIVE BONUS

## 40 Weight Loss Recipes

## &

## 14 Days Meal Plan

Scan the QR-Code and receive
the FREE download:

Printed in Great Britain
by Amazon

29735376R00085